SCOTLAND – VEGETARIAN HEAVEN

Vegetarian Guides are the most comprehensive vegetarian guidebooks in the world, carried and relied on by tens of thousands of UK vegetarians since 1994, and recommended by all the leading vegetarian organisations and magazines.

The books offer vegans, vegetarians, meat reducers, their partners and families a huge choice of places where everyone will enjoy a delicious, memorable and great value night out or weekend away.

Featuring...

32 vegetarian restaurants, cafes and pubs
118 more restaurants, cafes and pubs that veggies and vegans love
15 vegetarian accommodation
41 more places to stay with great veggie grub
114 delis, wholefood and other stores where local veggies shop
Vegetarian caterers
Local vegetarian groups to meet new friends

See what's in your area:

	Places to stay		Places to eat			
	Veggie	Omni	Veggie	Omni	Shops	Page
Edinburgh	1	9	13	24	17	1
Glasgow		6	8	20	33	35
Lowlands	6	16	6	48	51	71
Highlands	3	6	2	20	10	129
Islands	5	4	3	8	4	143
TOTAL	**15**	**41**	**32**	**120**	**115**	

D0488364

For latest open
www.vegetarianguides.co.uk/updates

The perfect present for vegetarians, vegans, meat reducers and those who love them (but never knew where to take them)

Vegetarian Scotland, 1st edition

by Alex Bourke & Ronny Worsey
ISBN 978-1-902259-13-0

Published January 2012 by Vegetarian Guides Ltd,
PO Box 2284, London W1A 5UH, England
www.vegetarianguides.co.uk   info@vegetarianguides.co.uk
Tel 020-3239 8433 (24 hours)   Fax 0870-288 5085 skype veggie_guides

UK & worldwide Distribution: Bertrams, Bookspeed,
Gardners, Green City, Highland Wholefoods, Suma
USA/Canada distribution: Book Publishing Company, TN

Design and maps: Mickaël Charbonnel, Alexandra Boylan,
Andrea Mattioli, Rudy Penando & Jenny Carp
Vegetarian Guides logo design: Marion Gillet
Copy-editing/proofreading: Catherine Laurence

Cover photos (clockwise from top left)
1. Tapa Bakehouse, Edinburgh
2. Edinburgh from Carlton Hill
3. The 13th Note vegetarian pub, Glasgow
4. Loch Morlich watersports centre
5. Henderson's shop & deli, Edinburgh
6. Vegan vet Andrew Knight in the Cairngorms (by Jasmijn de Boo)
2,4,6 © www.andrewsadventures.info, where you can enjoy heaps more photos
of Scotland and the world by vegan adventurers Andrew Knight and Jasmijn de Boo

Printed and bound in Great Britain by QNS, Newcastle upon Tyne
www.qnsprint.co.uk

Join the team: If you have updates, or a group, shop or cafe and want copies to resell or give as gifts, we will do you a very attractive discount. Contact updates@ or sales@vegetarianguides.co.uk or call us on (+44) (0)20-3239 8433 (24 hours, we call back).

Disclaimer: Restaurants are continually changing their owners and opening hours and sometimes close for holidays. Every effort has been made to ensure the accuracy of information in this book, however it is impossible to account for every detail and mistakes can occur. Before making a special journey, we recommend you call ahead to check details.

Vegetarian Britain 4th edition
part 8:
SCOTLAND

Edinburgh, Glasgow, Aberdeen, Angus, Argyll, Ayrshire, Borders, Fife, Morayshire, Perthshire, Stirlingshire, Highlands and Islands

300 places to eat, sleep and shop veggie

by Alex Bourke & Ronny Worsey
with special thanks to
Amanda Baker, Chris Childe, George Rodger

Contributors:

Edinburgh: Gemma Learmonth, Andrew Richards, Bani Sethi

Glasgow: Paul Philbrow, Gemma Learmonth, Athene Richford, Patricia Tricker

Aberdeenshire: Andy Oliver, George Rodger

Angus: Barry Constable, Laura Lawson

Argyll: Ray Grant, Al Kingsbury, Chrissie Tucker

Ayrshire: Sylvia Johnston McCosh

Borders: Karen Page

Fife: Chris Childe, Donna Paterson

Morayshire: Pam Bochel

Perth & Kinross: Chris Childe
Darren & Kate at Highland Health Store

Stirlingshre: Penny Veitch

Highlands: Pam Bochel, Chris Childe
Andrew Knight, Julia Ridgman, Vicky Shilling, Linda Seller

Islands: Amanda Baker, Jo Fox, Tracey Hague,
Andrew Knight, Catherine Laurence, Kim Shankar

 Vegetarian Guides

LEWIS
Stornoway

N. UIST
Uig
Dunvegan
Ullinish
Carbost
SKYE
Skeabost
Portree
Struan
Luib
Broadford
Kyle of
Lochalsh

S. UIST

BARRA

RUM

COLL

TIREE

MULL

IONA

ARGYLL
AND BUTE

Lochgilphead

Minard

Inverary

BUTE

ARRAN
Brodick
HOLY
ISLE

KINTYRE

Durness

Lochinver

Ullapool

WESTER ROSS

Dingwall

Drumnadrochit

HIGHLAND
Loch Ness

Kingussie
Newtonmore

Fort William
Onish
Ben Nevis

Tyndrum

Lochearnhead

STIRLING
Loch
Lomond
Balfron
Station

Ayr

Kilmarnoch

AYRSHIRE

Maybole

Moniaive

Girvan

Pinwherry

Stranraer

John O'Groats

Thurso

SUTHERLAND

Lairg

Rogart Station

Dornoch

EASTER ROSS

Cromarty
Findhorn

Nairn
Forres

Inverness

MORAY

Nethy Bridge

Aviemore

ORKNEYS
and
SHETLANDS

ABERDEENSHIRE
Aberdeen

ANGUS

Dundee

PERTH
AND
KINROSS

Perth

Cupar
St Andrews

Falkland

FIFE

Glenrothes

Dunfermline

Kirkcaldy

Glasgow

Lochwinnoch

LANARKSHIRE

LOTHIAN

Edinburgh

Lumsdaine
Chirnside

Berwick-upon-
Tweed

SCOTTISH
BORDERS

NORTHUMBERLAND

DUMFRIES AND GALLOWAY
Dumfries
New Abbey

CUMBRIA

1. GLASGOW CITY
2. EAST RENFREWSHIRE
3. RENFREWSHIRE
4. INVERCLYDE

Vegetarian Scotland: Contents

VEGETARIAN RESTAURANTS, CAFES & PUBS

*all food vegan

VEGETARIAN ACCOMMODATION

If self-catering, or even if not, to avoid having to carry supplies, check out **Highland Wholefoods** in Inverness (pages 137-8). You can order from them or one of the many shops they supply all over Scotland and your order will be waiting at a shop when you arrive, or can be delivered to your accommodation. Remember shops may get a weekly delivery, so contact them at least a week before. Any wholefood store should be able to order in for you.

Quirky and Special Places

The Engine Shed, Edinburgh
There are limited opening hours, but awesome value all-veggie food in this community enterprise staffed by people with learning difficulties. They make the best smoked tofu we've ever tasted (photo right). Page 13.

The Piemaker, Edinburgh
Most pie shops are out of bounds to vegans, but this Edinburgh institution offers clearly-labelled sweet and savoury options including Thai mushroom and a maple syrup lattice. The long opening hours are a real bonus. Page 21.

Mono, Glasgow
If you like to groove while you scoff and sup, visit Mono, a cafe-bar with a built-in record shop. The place also doubles up as a gig venue in the evenings. The menu is all vegan and they brew their own ginger beer on site. If we could teleport, we'd be there. Page 46.

Tchai-Ovna House of Tea, Glasgow
Fancy an unusual brew? You won't be limited to Assam, Darjeeling and Co-op 99 in this tea emporium, which sells over 80 varieties, from Golden Dragon Jasmine to Oolong Wu-long. There's veggie nosh and poetry nights, too. Page 53.

The Findhorn Foundation, Morayshire
This long-established place on two sites manages to be an ecological village, a music venue, a spiritual retreat, an education centre, a caravan park, a vegetarian-friendly cafe and lots of other things. It's home to hundreds of people and welcomes thousands of paying visitors each year. Page 115.

Ullapool, Wester Ross
This tiny coastal town has a surprisingly mild climate, with palm trees. The mountains run right down to the harbour. Despite its remote location, the place is a mecca for book, music and art lovers, with festivals and events all year round. There are also two vegetarian bed and breakfasts. Pages 132, 141.

Sleeperzzz, Sutherland
Wake up to stunning views from the windows of this self-catering hostel in a train carriage. You'll find castles, distilleries and mountain-bike trails nearby.

Itadaki Zen vegan Japanese restaurant, Oban, Argyll

Bonnie Scotland!

Like the cinema adverts say: visit Scotland!

Scottish people don't wear sporrans down the pub, toss cabers, dance around in kilts (except at weddings) or set fire to wicker men on beaches. The roads don't peter out into gravel tracks north of Carlisle. You won't get savaged by a million marauding midges *every* time you venture outdoors, and there's a lot more on the drinks menu than whisky (marvellous though it is).

Scotland is a beautiful, forward-thinking country full of friendly people and packed with great places to visit. Although it has a long-standing reputation for an abundance of battered, deep-fried stodgy food, you'll also find a wide range of fresh, quality dishes from around the world, especially in Edinburgh and Glasgow.

Organic and healthy foods are really taking off in Scotland, with lots of low fat eating initiatives being in schools and new wholefood shops popping up all the time. You'll be amazed at the sheer range of tasty and imaginative meals and snacks.

Glasgow is a cosmopolitan, ethnically-diverse and fun place, with more vegetarian pubs than anywhere else in Europe (four of them have vegan menus, in fact!). It has a big arts scene, with live gigs everywhere, and some of the best architecture in Britain. You'll miss out on a lot if you don't pay a visit.

Edinburgh is the number one tourist destination in Scotland, especially during August, when the population soars due to all the coinciding festivals. It's worth a visit all year round due to the sheer rugged beauty of the place, the range and quality of the restaurants, and the many attractions such as the castle and the Scottish History Museum, which I rate as one of the best I've ever visited.

Many tourists leave the cities behind to visit Loch Ness in search of the monster, **Loch Lomond** for the views, the **West Highlands** and the **Cairngorms** to hike up mountains, and the many **gorgeous islands like Skye** and **Rum** to get away from it all. These areas have fewer taste-bud sensations for veggies, but you'll still be well catered for. There's a wide range of accommodation to suit you all, from honeymooning couples on the spend, to backpacking students on a tight budget.

If you're a **stone circle** freak like me, you'll find plenty of neolithic sites in Aberdeenshire, where the Picts once ruled. Unlike southern England, where sites are ring-fenced and admission fees levied, the sites are free to visit and untainted by vandals.

Finally, a word on the **weather**. Yeah, Scotland tends to be a few degrees cooler than the rest of Britain. The North East has chilly, bracing winds, though unknown to many, it also has a dry, sunny climate, with lower rainfall than London. North West Scotland is milder and damper, so dress for drizzle all year round. Midges can be an annoying problem in summer in the mountains, though you won't see them in towns or right on the coast. Check the midge forecast afore ye go.

– Ronny

Vegetarian Scotland

A holiday in Britain is not complete without visiting Scotland. The Highlands are breathtaking, the people are incredibly friendly, and the cities throb with life and culture.

Scotland has a slightly different **legal system** to that of England and Wales. Public access to the countryside is relatively unrestricted, with walking over uncultivated land and wild camping both being legal (provided no damage is caused, fires lit or litter dropped, of course!).

Top of the list of places to visit is Edinburgh, the capital. From the ancient castle, museums and galleries to the many pubs and night clubs, you will never be without something to see or do. The famous Fringe Festival, International Festival, Military Tattoo and Book Festival take over the city every August, so get in quick if booking accommodation for that month. You will not go hungry in this city. Edinburgh is excellent for vegetarians and vegans. **The number of vegetarian restaurants just keeps on growing** and it now rivals London as being the best city in Britain for vegetarian eating. Even if you are at an omnivorous restaurant, in Edinburgh they are used to catering for veggies and most know how to knock up a great meat-free meal.

Don't leave Scotland before you check out **Glasgow, the country's largest city. It is lively and cosmopolitan with a more 'Scottish' feel** than Edinburgh, and eating out is generally cheaper.

Glasgow was the first modern city in the West to be laid out in a grid and was the model for many of the American cities. It was recently used as an American city for a Hollywood movie. Glasgow is particularly known for its architecture due to Charles Mackintosh (1868–1928), the famous Glasgow-born architect and designer, who is renowned world wide for his innovative style which helped shape European Art Nouveau. Glasgow has a big shopping centre, a huge street market and loads of cosy cafes, bars and live music venues. Although not quite the vegetarian paradise that Edinburgh is, Glasgow is catching up fast and is the only city in Europe with an incredible **six vegetarian and vegan food pubs**: Mono, Stereo, The 78, The 13th Note, Heavenly and Saramago at CCA.

Aberdeen is Britain's northernmost city and it has a very distinct look, due to most of the buildings being made from granite, which sparkles in the sun. Aberdeen does not have any gourmet vegetarian restaurants, but do check out the bargain **all-vegan Tropical Gateway cafe**. A number of other places have good veggie options and the city gets better for eating out each year.

If you love Scottish **malt whisky**, be sure to visit a distillery. Most welcome visitors and offer guided tours, for which they'll charge anything from £2 to £6 per person. This normally includes a complimentary 'drammie' and a money-off voucher that you can redeem against a purchase from the shop, so if you intend to buy a bottle, the tour is effectively free.

If stunning scenery is what you're after, be sure to visit the **North West Highlands**. Once you get north of Glen Coe, the roads become narrow and the views are incredible, with beautiful mountains and valleys everywhere you look, especially in the Sutherland area. **Fort William** and **Aviemore** are popular ski resorts and although sadly lacking vegetarian restaurants, you can still find decent food. You can't go wrong in an Italian or Indian restaurant and you will find both in these towns.

North East Scotland is less dramatic, but has lots of attractive hills and mountains covered in swathes of purple heather, herds of stags, red squirrels and pine forests. This part of Scotland boasts a huge number of well-preserved neolithic sites that are generally free to visit, such as stone circles dating back 5,000 years – that's older than the pyramids! The **Cairngorms National Park** near Aberdeen is a very popular destination for walkers and skiers.

If you fancy a day out with a difference, try a tour of the **Black Isle Brewery** in Ross-shire: their beers are all vegetarian and organic. Close by is the **Findhorn Foundation** – a huge eco-community that runs a range of courses each year. They have a music venue with a veggie-friendly cafe that hosts acts from around the world.

All over Scotland there are vegetarian guesthouses in small towns or the remote and beautiful countryside. Imagine waking in the morning to the smell of vegetarian bacon and scrambled tofu, hearing the sound of birds chirping and knowing that all you have to do that day is enjoy yourself. Your Scottish hosts will do their utmost to ensure that you do.

For general tourist information on Scotland go to:
www.visitscotland.com
ww.scotland-info.co.uk
www.undiscoveredscotland.co.uk
www.wildlife.visitscotland.com
www.snh.gov.uk – Scottish Natural Heritage

Scotland what's on guide:
www.whatshappeningon.com

Scottish Vegans discussion forum:
http://groups.yahoo.com/group/scottishvegans/
They meet monthly for a potluck lunch in members' homes.

How to attract vegans
to your hotel or bed and breakfast
and keep them coming back

If you're a B&B owner, have a read.
If you're a traveller, try showing this page to your hosts.

Most vegan guests aren't fussy – we just want our custom to be respected as much as everybody else's, especially if we're paying the same. A few simple gestures can turn our stay into an enjoyable experience that we'll tell our friends about. Here are some suggestions:

Always have soya milk for cereals and hot drinks. It costs about the same as UHT cows' milk from supermarkets and will keep for months in a cupboard and for up to a week when opened. You can also use it in the same way as cows' milk to make custard, bechamel sauce and rice pudding.

Linda McCartney sausages are vegan, but Quorn ones aren't. Many types of frozen **hash browns** are vegan, as are baked beans and most breads.

Don't just offer us a full Scottish breakfast without the meat and eggs, as it probably won't be worth eating. It's simple enough to make vegan potato scones, buy in vegan sausages (or make your own) and knock up some scrambled tofu. Combined with mushrooms, tomatoes, hash browns, toast and beans, you can give us a feast we'll be grateful for.

A simple, but effective, light breakfast option is fried or grilled vine tomatoes on toast with a drizzle of olive oil. You can also make porridge the proper Scottish way, of course, with water and a pinch of salt.

Many mainstream breakfast cereals are vegan, such as Cornflakes, Weetabix, Rice Krispies, Bran Flakes, Ready Brek and Coco Pops.

Hummus is available everywhere and is a versatile sandwich ingredient. **If you use dairy-free margarine as standard, it is suitable for just about everybody.** Common brands are Vitalite and Pure. You can also buy egg-free mayonnaise in supermarkets.

Many types of biscuit are vegan, such as almost every brand of bourbons, fig rolls and ginger nuts. Jammie Dodgers and plain Hob Nobs are also vegan.

Leather sofas can make us feel uncomfortable, as can down-filled duvets. If you have such fittings, it's a good idea to mention it when we book, so we can make an informed choice.

You can get a wide range of vegan products from both wholefood shops and supermarkets. Wholesalers like 3663 carry a smaller range.

Ronny has over 10 years' catering experience and loves a good breakfast.

Do you love cakes?

Are you any of the following? A vegan, a trainee vegan, someone who lives with a vegan, a kitchen scientist, a student, a cartoon lover, a lazy cook or a vegetarian wanting to ride the 'cool wave'?

Do you like the sound of the following? Chocolate Eclairs, Foxy Brownies, Bakewell Slice, White Chocolate Carrot Cake, Tiffin, Vanilla Pecan Parcels, Cinder Toffee and Rum 'n' Raisin Sponge Pudding.

If so, you need the brand new 20 page cookbook:

Return of the Cake Scoffer

Available now from Vegetarian Guides for £1.50, see end pages

Wholesale orders visit www.activedistribution.org
Bulk orders (50+) at a big discount, contact the publisher: **scoffer@chef.net**
or write to: Scoffer Towers, c/o 245 Gladstone St, Nottingham NG7 6HX

Beer and Pubs

by Sagar Kirit Shah of **Real Ale For All** *&* **Ronny Worsey**

Beer and cider production, like wine, often involves animal products in the fining process to help remove impurities and improve the appearance of the final product. Fining aids include fish isinglass (a collagen from the swim bladder), gelatine, egg whites or casein. Unfortunately this makes many beers non-vegetarian, especially ales.

EU and UK legislation does not require breweries to list ingredients in any drinks with an alcoholic content of more than 1.2% volume – so usually you don't know by the label if it is vegetarian or vegan. This is unlikely to change in the future, as many breweries and wine-makers are fighting hard to keep the law as it is, so customers will not see all the chemicals they use.

Fortunately, many cask and keg beers and ciders are animal-free and use either bentonite (a type of clay) or pea extract, or are left longer to settle. Unlike wines, popular beers and ciders are generally branded clearly and it is nearly always possible to find some in a pub or supermarket.

Bottle-conditioned real ales are almost always vegan because they are not filtered. Yeast needs to be in the bottle in order for it to continue fermenting. The same applies to cloudy ciders.

As a general rule, **cask-conditioned ales** (and even many bottled ales) are not suitable for vegetarians or vegans. Real Ale For All (RAFA) has been working with the Vegan Society to encourage breweries to go vegan but this may take a long time. Lagers and ciders are more likely to be veggie as they are generally chill-filtered, or left for much longer to settle.

Some Scottish brands wear their veggie credentials on their sleeve, such as Black Isle Brewery, whose beers are also organic, and Williams Brothers, who produce Fraoch heather beer and Alba pine and spruce beer. Vegan bottled ales (at the time of going to print) that are widely available in British supermarkets and off-licences include Batemans, Badger, Black Sheep, Brakspear, Bridge of Allan, Cain's, Caledonian, Charles Wells, Co-op, Duchy Originals, Freedom, Fullers, Hoegaarden, Sam Smiths, Shepherd Neame and Wychwood. Plus all German brands and most supermarket own-brands.

These websites list many popular beers and ciders and indicate whether they are suitable for vegetarians and/or vegans. The first one displays emails and letters received from breweries so you can verify the info.

www.barnivore.com
www.veggiewines.co.uk
www.vegansociety.com/AFSSearch.aspx
www.enchant.me.uk/Vegetarian_beers.html (a bit old)

BEER YES

Becks, Brakspear
Budweiser
Carlsberg, Cobra
Grolsch
Heineken
Hoegaarden
Holsten Pils
Lowenbrau
Miller
Shepherd Neame
Stella Artois

BEER NO

Boddingtons
Carling, Fosters
Greene King
Guinness
John Smiths
Kronenbourg
Newcastle Brown
Red Stripe
San Miguel
Staropramen
Tetleys

CIDER YES

Magners pear cider
Scrumpy Jack
Strongbow
Westons
Woodpecker

CIDER NO

Blackthorn
Diamond White
Kopparberg
Magners apple cider
Strongbow Sirrus

Source: www.veggiewines.co.uk & The Vegan Society

The **Wetherspoons** chain of over 700 pubs sells several vegan beers and ciders and normally have a vegetarin dish which can be made vegan. It used to be chickpea and spinach curry, lately hummus and roast veg wrap with baked potato.

The **Sam Smiths** pub chain sells a variety of beers from their own breweries at affordable prices, and 90% are certified with the Vegan Society, though they do not offer vegan food. www.samsmiths.info

The 13th Note, page 42. Food is vegan by default, unless marked V for vegetarian. Alcohol includes vegan options.

Meanwhile in **Edinburgh** a good bet for a pint is **The Auld Hoose, page 18,** which does some great veggie and vegan pub grub.

Many breweries produce vegan beer and offer tours. We can recommend a visit to the **Little Black Isle Brewery** near Inverness.

Glasgow Vegetarian Pubs

The 78, page 44. All food and alcohol vegan.
Mono, page 46. Food, all wine and most beer vegan.
Stereo, page 48. Food vegan except option of cow's milk in hot drinks. Some beers vegan but not all as they're tied to a brewery.
Heavenly, page 50. Food, house wines and all beers except Fosters vegan.
Saramago at CCA, page 52. Food vegan except cow's milk in hot drinks. Some alcohol such as Guinness not vegan.

For Ronny's online guide to vegetarian wine:
www.vegetarianguides.co.uk/wine

To find out if your favourite drink is
suitable for vegetarians or vegans consult:
www.barnivore.com
www.veggiewines.co.uk
www.vegansociety.com/AFSSearch.aspx
www.enchant.me.uk/Vegetarian_beers.html

For a guide to vegetarian wine:
www.vegetarianguides.co.uk/wine

The information on this card is provided in good faith based on information supplied by
veggiewines.co.uk and the Vegan Society in August 2010, who have contacted the
manufacturers. Vegetarian Guides cannot be held liable for any inaccuracy. You
are advised to make your own enquiries to confirm the latest situation.
www.vegetarianguides.co.uk

BEER YES

Becks, Brakspear
Budweiser
Carlsberg, Cobra
Grolsch
Heineken
Hoegaarden
Holsten Pils
Lowenbrau
Miller
Shepherd Neame
Stella Artois

BEER NO

Boddingtons
Carling, Fosters
Greene King
Guinness
John Smiths
Kronenbourg
Newcastle Brown
Red Stripe
San Miguel
Staropramen
Tetleys

CIDER YES

Magners pear cider
Scrumpy Jack
Strongbow
Westons
Woodpecker

CIDER NO

Blackthorn
Diamond White
Kopparberg
Magners apple cider
Strongbow Sirrus

Source: www.veggiewines.co.uk & The Vegan Society

VEGETARIAN SHOES

*I don't eat the inside and I won't wear the
outside.* Pick up non-leather shoes and
walking boots at:

www.beyondskin.co.uk (heels heels heels)
www.bboheme.com
www.ethicalwares.com
www.freerangers.com
www.neoncollective.com
www.veganline.com
www.vegetarian-shoes.co.uk

Edinburgh is one of the most attractive and striking cities in Britain, with stunning stone buildings overlooked by an imposing castle, and centuries of history and culture.

The city centre is full of lively pubs, cafes and shops, and is as good as Brighton and London for vegetarian food. Walking around requires a degree of fitness, as the city is very hilly and parts of the centre set on two levels, which adds to its atmosphere and rugged good looks. There are several excellent free museums, along with a thriving arts scene. The botanical gardens are also well worth a visit.

The annual Edinburgh Fringe Festival, International Festival, Book Festival and Military Tattoo draw thousands of people, so if you are planning to visit during late July or August, book your accommodation as far in advance as possible and expect to pay more than usual.

www.edinburghdaysout.com
www.edinburgh.org
www.edinburghcastle.gov.uk
www.edinburghcastle.biz
www.edinburgh-inspiringcapital.com

Websites recommended by Claymore Vegetarian Guest House:
www.edinburghsparkles.com
www.edinburghschristmas.com
www.edinburghguide.com/festival/edinburghswinterfestivals
www.informededinburgh.co.uk
www.edinburghspotlight.com
www.list.co.uk

Edinburgh

Best places in Edinburgh for:

A romantic dinner – David Bann

Relaxing with tea and cake – The Edinburgh Larder

A quick, heathy bite on a budget – The Engine Shed

A brew and a chat– The Elephant House

Taking a big group of mates – Chop Chop

A celebration feast with a difference – Black Bo's

All–day breakfast with a pint – The Auld Hoose

A healthy Sunday afternoon – Henderson's Bistro

Student scoffing– The Baked Potato Shop

Sitting outdoors – Henderson's @St John's

Taking the kids – Filmhouse Cafe

Taking a dog – Earthy Market Cafe, Southside

Ethical credentials – Himalaya Shop and Cafe

Breakfast at Claymore vegetarian guest house

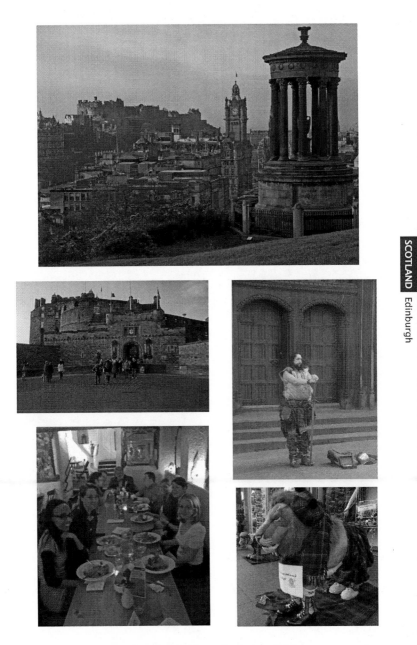

Around Edinburgh *(photos by Andrew Knight)*

3

VEGETARIAN EDINBURGH

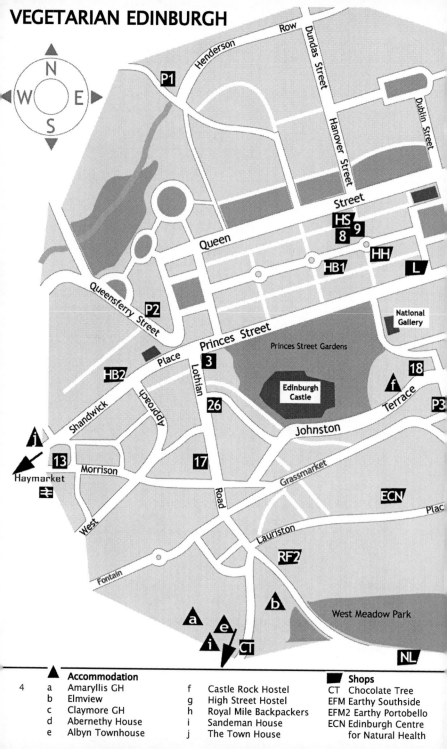

N W E S

P1

Henderson Row
Dundas Street
Hanover Street
Dublin Street

Queen Street

HS 9
8

HB1 HH

L

Queensferry Street

P2

National Gallery

Princes Street

Princes Street Gardens

Place
Lothian
3

HB2

Edinburgh Castle

18

f

Terrace

P3

26

Approach
Shandwick

i

13

Morrison

West

Johnston

17

Road

Grassmarket

ECN
Plac

Lauriston

RF2

Fontain

a

e

i

g

b

West Meadow Park

NL

Accommodation

4
- a Amaryllis GH
- b Elmview
- c Claymore GH
- d Abernethy House
- e Albyn Townhouse
- f Castle Rock Hostel
- g High Street Hostel
- h Royal Mile Backpackers
- i Sandeman House
- j The Town House

Shops

- CT Chocolate Tree
- EFM Earthy Southside
- EFM2 Earthy Portobello
- ECN Edinburgh Centre
       for Natural Health

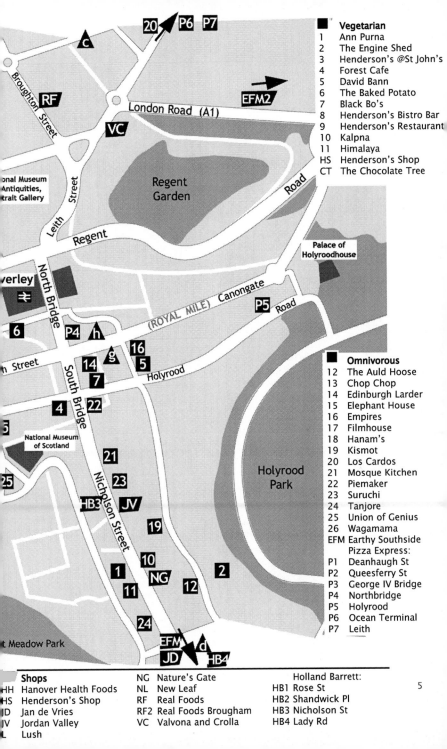

Vegetarian
1 Ann Purna
2 The Engine Shed
3 Henderson's @St John's
4 Forest Cafe
5 David Bann
6 The Baked Potato
7 Black Bo's
8 Henderson's Bistro Bar
9 Henderson's Restaurant
10 Kalpna
11 Himalaya
HS Henderson's Shop
CT The Chocolate Tree

Omnivorous
12 The Auld Hoose
13 Chop Chop
14 Edinburgh Larder
15 Elephant House
16 Empires
17 Filmhouse
18 Hanam's
19 Kismot
20 Los Cardos
21 Mosque Kitchen
22 Piemaker
23 Suruchi
24 Tanjore
25 Union of Genius
26 Wagamama
EFM Earthy Southside
Pizza Express:
P1 Deanhaugh St
P2 Queesferry St
P3 George IV Bridge
P4 Northbridge
P5 Holyrood
P6 Ocean Terminal
P7 Leith

Shops
HH Hanover Health Foods
HS Henderson's Shop
JD Jan de Vries
JV Jordan Valley
L Lush

NG Nature's Gate
NL New Leaf
RF Real Foods
RF2 Real Foods Brougham
VC Valvona and Crolla

Holland Barrett:
HB1 Rose St
HB2 Shandwick Pl
HB3 Nicholson St
HB4 Lady Rd

5

Edinburgh accommodation

Claymore Vegetarian Guest House

Vegetarian guest house

68 Pilrig Street, Edinburgh EH6 5AS
Tel: 0131–554 2500
Open: all year except Xmas
Train: Waverley then bus 11, 5–10 mins
Bus: 11 from South St Davids Street to the door. 22, 25, 10, 16 from Princes Street, get off when you see the big church on the left half way down Leith Walk then 5 mins walk.
www.claymorevegetarianguesthouse.com
Facebook: Claymore Vegetarian Guest House
enquirehere@blueyonder.co.uk

Cathy and John welcome you to their veggie oasis in a central Victorian terraced house 15 minutes walk from Princes Street, or take the 11 bus which stops outside.

6 rooms, 3 ensuite. Prices per person doubles/twins from £35, family rooms (for 3 or 4) £30, single occupancy from £40. Higher rates in August aroud £50 per person, New Year and special events such as rugby weekends when there is a minimum stay of 3 nights. Low season Nov–Mar and midweek specials.

Full cooked vegetarian or vegan breakfast, plus cold buffet including cereals, soya yogurt, bakery.

Rooms have digital TV, tea/coffee making, hairdryer, wifi. Guests can use the house laptop. Children welcome. Plentiful street parking.

Abernethy House

Omnivorous bed & breakfast and self-catering accommodation

51 Findhorn Place, Grange, Edinburgh EH9 2NZ (20 minutes walk to the Old Town)
Tel: 0131-667 2526
Open: all year
Train: Waverley then bus 42 £1.30; taxi £6.50. Also bus 24 to West End.
www.lumison.co.uk/~marilyn_nicholl
abernethyhouse@ednet.co.uk

Self-contained garden level apartment (a few steps down) with double bed in a Victorian house where the owner really understands vegetarian, vegan and coeliac. £35-55 single, double £40-75, depending on season and length of stay. Bathroom with bath and shower. Cooked or continental breakfast as you wish. Tea and coffee making, hairdryer. Parking on/off street. Dogs welcome. Wifi. Dvd player and radio, dvds and books available.
Up to date info on the city and events available from owner. French and German spoken. Guitar, violin and trombone available. Counselling, coaching and Person Centred Therapy available.
Earthy organic store and Earthy Market Cafe are 2 minutes walk at 33-41 Ratcliffe Terrace, see shops section. Nearby are Indian and Chinese restaurants with take-away and an excellent pub.

Albyn Townhouse

Omnivorous guesthouse

16 Hartington Gardens, Edinburgh EH10 4LD
Tel: 0131-229 6459
Fax: 0131-228 5807
Open: all year
Train: Waverley or Haymarket (closest) then taxi £7 or walk 15 minutes
www.albyntownhouse.co.uk
info@albyntownhouse.co.uk

Big 4 star guesthouse in a quiet street, next door to what used to be the Greenhouse vegetarian guesthouse (alas closed 2010). They get lots of repeat customers, mainly couples and families. Generous full cooked vegetarian or vegan breakfast, or porridge on request. 10 ensuite rooms: 2 family (up to 3 or 4 people), 5 kingsize double, 3 twin/double. Nov-Mar £79 per room (£55 as single), April to Oct £89, Jul-Aug £110 (no singles), New Year : £120 (4 nights minimum). Minimum two nights at weekends.
Room have TV, tea and coffee making, hairdryer and radio/alarm clock. Ironing facilities are available. Baby cot available. Private car park. No pets.

Amaryllis Guest House

Omnivorous guest house

21 Upper Gilmore Place, Edinburgh EH3 9NL
Tel: 0131-229 3293
Open: all year
www.amaryllisguesthouse.com
amaryllisguesthouse@blueyonder.co.uk

Early 1800's Georgian townhouse in a quiet residential street, with five rooms for 2 to 6 people. Single £45-55, double or triple £30-45 per person, family £30-40 per person. Vegetarian and vegan breakfast available 8.30-9.00a.m, just tell them what you'd like and they'll get it for you, Real Foods (Brougham) is nearby.

Private parking for 2 cars so you need to reserve it. Rooms have tea/coffee, tv. Hairdryers and ironing available. City and Highlands tours arranged. MC, Visa.

Elmview

Omnivorous bed and breakfast

15 Glengyle Terrace, Edinburgh, EH3 9LN
Tel: 0131–228 1973
Open: 1st April – 31st October
www.elmview.co.uk

A luxurious five star bed and breakfast that's used to catering for vegetarians. 5 large ensuite double rooms, of which 4 can be converted into twins. Prices range from £45 per person in April to £65 in August. Single people pay £15 less per room (£75–115). Rooms have a sofa and hairdryer, wifi, tea and coffee making and drawers full of useful things like scissors and sewing kits.

Dietary requirements should be stated on booking but you'll be well catered for, with vegan breakfast options like blueberry pancakes with maple syrup, strawberries with soya yoghurt, porridge and cereals.

No pets, smoking or children under 15.

Sandeman House

Omnivorous bed and breakfast

33 Colinton Road, Merchiston, Edinburgh, EH10 5DR
Tel: 0131–447 8080
Open: all year
www.sandemanhouse.co.uk

A small bed and breakfast a mile south of Edinburgh Castle, with 2 en-suite double rooms and 1 twin. Prices range from £40–£65 (double) and £60–75 (single) per person, depending on time of year and how many nights you want to stay. Discounts for longer stays.

All rooms have wifi, digital tv and tea and coffee making.

Breakfast includes seasonal fruit and jams from their own allotment, home-made vegetable cutlets and potato scones. If you're vegan just say so when booking, and they'll provide soya yogurt and vegan sausages.

Accept all cards except American Express. No pets, smoking or children under 8 (except by arrangement).

The Town House

Omnivorous bed and breakfast

65 Gilmore Place, Edinburgh, EH3 9NU
Tel: 0131–229 1985
Open: all year except Xmas and New Year
www.thetownhouse.com

A beautiful four star house less than 10 minutes' walk from Haymarket Station. Five ensuite rooms: 3 double, 1 twin, 1 single, from £45 (January) to £60 (August) per person per night. Hairdryers, tea and coffee makers and wifi in all rooms.

Breakfast options include cereal, fruit, porridge; and a fry-up of mushrooms, tomatoes, potato scones and beans. The owner is happy to buy in things on request, such as vegan sausages and soya milk.

No smoking throughout. No pets or children under 10.

The following vegetarian guest houses listed in earlier books have now closed: Greenhouse, Six Marys Place, No. 1.

Short let serviced apartments:
www.the–edinburgh–apartment.com

Castle Rock Hostel

Omnivorous hostel

15 Johnston Terrace, Edinburgh EH1 2PW
Tel: 0131-225 9666
Open: all year, 24 hours
Train: Waverley, 10 minutes' walk
www.castlerockedinburgh.com

Next to the castle on a quiet street, this ornate and lavishly-furnished hostel has almost 300 beds. There are both single sex and mixed dorms which have 8-16 beds and cost as little as £12 per night, £14 weekend, £17 August. Quad room (4 friends sharing) £15-17 per person; double room from £45 per night. No private rooms. No school groups or stag/hen groups.

Veggie continental breakfast £1.80 for cereal, juice and roll. Free tea and coffee. If you're vegan, you'll need to bring your own soya milk and margarine. Big communal kitchen with fridges.

Coal fires in winter. Internet 80p/half hour, free wifi. Lockers in rooms with keys. Good recycling facilities.

High Street Hostel

Omnivorous hostel

8 Blackfriars Street, Edinburgh EH1 1NE
Tel: 0131-557 3984
Open: all year, 24 hours
Train: Waverley, 5 minutes walk
www.highstreethostel.com

A gorgeous building dating from 1564 with a colourful interior, in a small street off the Royal Mile in the heart of the Old Town. 140 beds from £11 (midweek, winter) to £16 (weekend, summer) in a single sex dorm of 6 to 16 people. The price inreases to £22.50 in August. Also quad rooms £10 per person Sun-Thu, £16 weekend, and one double and two twin rooms £40, £45 weekend.

Veggie continental breakfast £1.90. Free tea and coffee. If you're vegan, you'll need to bring your own soya milk and margarine. Kitchen for self-catering with fridges. Bedside lockers. No under-18s. Laundry service £3.50. Internet 80p/half hour, free wifi.

Royal Mile Backpackers

Omnivorous hostel

105 High Street, Edinburgh EH1 1SG
Tel: 0131-557 6120
Open: all year, reception open 06.30-23.00, then night porter till 03.00, but you can still get in by going to the sister High Street Hostel who will pop round to let you in
Train: Waverley, 10 minutes' walk
www.royalmilebackpackers.com

46 beds around £12 per night depending on time of year, but £27.50 in August, in a dorm of 8 to 10. Female and mixed dorms. Reductions for long stays. No private rooms. Lockers with keys. Towel hire 20p. No children.

Veggie continental breakfast £1.90. If you're vegan, you'll need to bring your own soya milk and margarine. Newly refurbished kitchen for self-catering with fridges, dining area, free tea and coffee.

Free wifi. Internet cafe nearby. Laundry service £3.50. Long term luggage storage 50p/day or £5/month.

The Baked Potato

Not just your usual spud! Very friendly small vegetarian take-away with one table located just off the Royal Mile, in the heart of Edinburgh, and a favourite of local students.

Good value, with small potatoes starting from £3.45. Fillings include pasta salad, rice peppers, Mexican, spinach or avocado salad and couscous. They do a superb vegan coleslaw. Hot fillings such as vegetarian haggis, chilli, vegetable curry or baked beans.

Varied selection of filled rolls, £1.80, and filled pittas from £2.50, with the same fillings as the potatoes, plus pates such as baba ghanoush or auberine and lentil. Tasty vegan sausage rolls too, £1.20 cold or £1.40 hot.

They make their own high quality vegan cakes (carrot, chocolate, cranberry and apple) which start from £1.10. Flapjacks 70p.

Coffee, tea and herb teas £1, they have soya milk. Organic cans £1.20, flavoured soya milks 70p. No alcohol.

Vegan mayonnaise and margarine available. Some gluten-free, wheat-free and raw foods

Lots of flyers for various holistic things and happenings and also leaflets on animal issues.

It can get very busy at lunchtime so expect lively crowds. The one table gets snapped up, so expect to take away.

56 Cockburn Street
Royal Mile
Edinburgh EH1 1PB

Tel: 0131-225 7572

Train: Waverley

Open: Mon-Sun 9.00-21.00
Extended hours during
Edinburgh festival (Mon-Sun
23.00)

Cash or cheque only

vegetarian – Edinburgh SCOTLAND

David Bann Restaurant

Vegetarian restaurant

Situated just off the Royal Mile, a combination of modern, minimalist décor with candlelight makes this elegant gourmet eatery popular with tourists and locals.

The international menu starts with snacks and starters from £3.60–£7.65 and main meals around £10–13. Dishes include Thai fritters with smoked tofu; chilli crepe with griddled courgette and chocolate sauce; risotto with roasted tomato, peas and basil; asparagus risotto; koftas; Japanese style tofu and veg stir-fry with shitake mushrooms and udon noodles.

There are lots of desserts for £5.60 or have an assiette of several desserts for two to share for £9. Vegan options include raspberries in jelly with orange drizzle cake and rum sorbet; or apple, pineapple and plums with amaretto marinated figs, served in a filo basket with homemade coconut rum sorbet.

House wine from £3.35 glass, £13.95 bottle. Unusual bottled beers £3.20–3.75 include Scottish heather ale and Ben Nevis organic ruby red beer.

Good range of drinks including a gorgeous foamy hot chocolate £2.30. Teas and coffees £1.90–2.30. Hot port with cloves £3.40. Fresh pressed fruit juices £2.

56–58 St Mary's Street
(Royal Mile and Cowgate)
Edinburgh EH1 1SX

Tel: 0131–556 5888

www.davidbann.com
Email: info@davidbann.co.uk

Open:
Sun–Thu 12.00–22.00
Fri–Sat 11.00–22.30

Children welcome, high chairs

MC, Visa

Booking recommended, except during August when they don't take them; arrive early!

SCOTLAND Edinburgh – vegetarian

Black Bo's

A funky, modern restaurant with an informal feel that's acclaimed for its unique, imaginative Cordon Vert dishes. They can adapt most dishes for gluten-free or vegan.

Starters £2.50–£6, include tofu and pistachio nori roulade with pomegranate, cassis and chillis; walnut, pumpkin and coriander pate with oatcakes; cashew and carrot roulade with midori sauce; and soup of the day with garlic bread.

Main courses £11.50–13.50 include potato, butter bean and leek roulade with cherry tomato and balsamic gravy. Few of the mains are vegan, though they can be adapted on request as food is prepared to order, such as spinach and walnut balls stufed with tofu and red pepper salsa.

Desserts £4–4.50 include vegan blueberry and frangipani tart, sorbets.

House wine £16.50 bottle, £3.25 small glass. Wines from around the world £16.50–26.50. Bottled beers from £3.60. Coffee £2. No soya milk. You don't have to eat to have a drink in the bar.

Vegetarian restaurant and bar

57–61 Blackfriars Street
Edinburgh EH1 1NB

Tel: 0131–557 6136

www.black-bos.com

Open:
Every day 18.00– 22.00, then bar stays open until 1am

Children welcome, no high chair

Gluten-free and special diets catered or adapted for

Bar attached, open to all.

MC, Visa

vegetarian – Edinburgh

SCOTLAND

Ann Purna

Vegetarian Indian Gujarati restaurant

45 St Patrick's Square, Edinburgh EH8 9ET
Tel: 0131-662 1807
Open: Mon–Sun 17.00–23.00

Local vegans tell us the food here is very nice, not drenched in oil like many Indian places, and they do a good vegan thali. They've spruced up the decor in recent years.

£4.95 for a 3-course lunch, £12–15 evenings. A meal could contain pakoras, bel poori or salad; vegetable curry or korma or mixed veg curry or dal; white or brown rice.

Desserts include fruit salad or strawberry, mango or carrot semolina halva. The staff are very vegan-aware.

House wine £12.95 bottle, £2.10 glass. Children most welcome, no high chairs. MC, Visa.

The Engine Shed Cafe

Vegetarian cafe

19 St Leonards Lane, Edinburgh EH8 9SD
Tel: 0131-662 0040
Open: Mon–Sat 10.00–16.00, Sun closed
www.theengineshed.org

Vegetarian cafe run as a social enterprise which trains people with learning disabilities. Light and airy, with big windows and lots of wooden fittings. Vegan options always available. They make their own amazing organic tofu (on sale here), bakery products, bread, pies etc which are on sale in some of the shops in Edinburgh and beyond.

Soup (always vegan) and roll £2.55. Mains £4.30 typically include chillis and casseroles. 6 or 8 salads (half vegan) including rice, couscous, £1.25 a portion, £3.25 for a plate of 3 salads, and £4.50 for a substantial mixed plate of 5 salads. Snacks £2.30–£3 such as sosage rolls, pies, fritata, falafel. Baked potato £1.80, with beans or two salads £2.85–3.20. Toasted focaccia filled roll such as hummus with antipasti, with salad £4.95.

Cakes £1.45 always include a vegan one such as chocolate cake. Tray bakes £1.25 such as apricot slices and cherry flapjacks.

Cold drinks £1–1.95 include juices, Belvoir sparkling drinks, Fentimans. Mug or pot of tea for one £1.15. Filter coffee £1.50. They have soya milk, but can't use it in capuccino or latte £1.80. Children welcome, high chairs. No dogs. MC, Visa, 3% charge on credit cards, 50p on debit cards under £10. Conference facilities and outside catering.

SCOTLAND Edinburgh – vegetarian

13

Henderson's Bistro Bar

Vegetarian cafe & bar

Cosy vegetarian cafe and bar above their restaurant. Vegan-friendly and a good option for eating out on a Sunday.

Soup £3.65. Patés £2.30. Salads £2.95-£4.50. Garlic bread £2.50. Wholemeal bruschetta with marinated wild mushrooms £4.20; wraps and grilled sandwiches.

Lunchtime mains £6-7, evening £8-9, include changing curries such as Thai with rice; Moroccan stew; vegan lasagne; haggis with clapshot (neeps and tatties); spicy beanburger with nachos, salsa and salad. Evening mains have additional options such as nut loaf.

Desserts £4.10-4.50 such as vegan wholemeal cherry pie or ginger and coconut cake.

25 Thistle Street
Edinburgh EH2 1DR

Tel: 0131-225 2605

hendersonsofedinburgh
.co.uk

Open:
Sun–Wed 12.00–20.30,
Thu–Sat 12.00–21.30

Children welcome, high chairs

Many biodynamic, organic and vegan wines. House wine £3.40 small glass, £4.95 large, £14.25 bottle.

MC, Visa

Henderson's Restaurant

Vegetarian canteen-style restaurant & wine bar

Formerly known as Henderson's Salad Table, this informal canteen-style place has been around since 1962, underneath the wholefood shop. They use seasonal, organic produce when possible, cater for special diets and have plenty of vegan options.

Before 11am full Scottish cooked breakfast £7.25 including coffee and juice. Porridge with soya milk and compote £3.60.

Lots of salads from £2.75. Four salads with bread £7.50. Up to 8 hot dishes which change daily, £5.95-6.95 lunch, £8.50-9.50 evening, such as baked pepper risotto, or burgers with salad and fried tortilla or veggies.

Desserts £3.95 with vegan options such as fresh or dried fruit salad, crumble, cherry pie, chocolate cake.

Fruit juices £1.75, fresh juices from £2.95. Teas £1.90 pot for one, Fairtrade filter coffee £1.95.

94 Hanover Street
Edinburgh EH2 1DR

Tel: 0131-225 2131

hendersonsofedinburgh
.co.uk

Open: Mon–Sat 8.00–22.00, Sun closed except Aug and Dec: 11.00–16.00/17.00

Children very welcome, high chairs

Organic house wine £3.65 glass, £14.50 bottle. Organic bottled beers and cider from £3.50.

10% discount for students

Outside catering. MC, Visa.

Henderson's @ St John's

Vegetarian cafe

3 Lothian Road, West End, Edinburgh EH4 3BJ
Open: Mon–Sat 10.00–17.00. Sun 11–16.00
Tel: 0131 229 0212
www.hendersonsofedinburgh.co.uk

Café in the basement of a church run by the same people as Henderson's bistro and restaurant. The premises were formerly Cornerstone Cafe, which started to serve fish, so it's great that it's veggie again. It has an excellent location on the corner of Princes Street and Lothian Road and views of the castle. 12 outside tables that seat up to 72 people, plus a simlar number indoors.

Soup and bread, £3.40, changes every day. Salads cost from £1.75. depending on how much of a plateful you have. mains £6.15 include veggie haggis with neeps and tatties; and baked potato with salad and risotto. Desserts £1.50–£3.25 include vegan apple and ginger cake; and pumpkin pie. Pot of tea for one £1.65. Coffees around £2. Organic wine and beer available. They always have soya milk. Gluten-free options.

Children welcome; nappy-changing facilities and high chairs.

Available for private hire. Outside catering available.

Henderson's Shop Deli

Vegetarian cafe and food shop with take-away counter

92 Hanover Street, Edinburgh EH2 1DR
Tel: 0131–225 6694
Open: Mon–Fri: 08.00–19.00, Sat 10.00–18.00, Sun 10.00–16.00
www.hendersonsofedinburgh.co.uk/deli.php

Above Henderson's Restaurant and next door to their Bistro (see earlier pages), this shop/deli (see later pages under Shops) also has a small cafe area with 12 seats. They do a lot of take-away with local offices, but it's quieter at the weekend especially Sunday.

Breakfast: organic porridge with soya milk £1.70 small, £1.90 large take-away or eat in.

Lunch: soups, pasties, pies, burgers, baked potatoes £2–£6.

Coffee £1.80 take-away, £1.95 large, £2.15 drink in.

The deli counter has hot and cold food with lots of organic, gluten-free and vegan options. Sandwiches, soups, pies, smoothies, juices and hot drinks to take away. Fridge with drinks, take-away salads, pasties, sandwiches, rolls, panini, hummus, tofu, soya yogurt.

For more about what they sell in the shop, see the Shops section below.

Forest Cafe

Arts centre and co-op veggie cafe

3 Bristo Place, Edinburgh EH11EY
Open: almost every day 10.00–23.00
http://blog.theforest.org.uk/cafe

This is the "alternative" place; a veggie cafe in an arts centre run by volunteers. At the time of printing, the owners of the building have gone bankrupt and the administrators forced the cafe out on 31st August 2011. The cafe collective has raised half of the £100,000 target to buy the building and now has the support of local members of parliament. See website if you want to support them, and for the latest status update. Here's the old menu: Main meals £5.40 such as burrito, falafel, or 3 salads with pitta. Daily specials such as curry or chilli with rice £5.35. Soup £3.10, with salad £5.30. Wraps £3.10. Pasties £2.55. Falafel burger £3.10. Chips and salsa or pitta and hummus £2.45. Cakes £1.85, slices £1.25, some vegan.

Tea £1, pot £1.45, for two £2.45, for three £3.40. Coffees and hot choc £1.25–2.25. Juice £1.15 half pint, £2.05 pint. Whole Earth cans £1.45. Bring your own booze and pay corkage 65p beer/cider, £1.40 wine. Kitchen staff are volunteers so tip generously.

Himalaya Shop and Cafe

Vegetarian cafe at the back of a shop

20 South Clerk Street, Edinburgh EH8 9PR
Tel: 0131–662 9818
Open: Every day 10.00–18.00 (plan to extend closing time to 20.00 as we go to print)
www.facebook.com/pages/
himalaya-shopcafe/299470156706

Cafe in the back of a small shop selling fair–trade gifts from India and Tibet, such as prayer bowls, wall hangings,

incense and jewellery. The project aims to raise awareness of Tibetan culture and to promote peace.

A chilled–out cafe with a mostly–vegan menu that sells big bowls of soup with bread for £3.35. Daily vegetable curry is £3.50. Cakes change every day according to who bakes and there's always vegan options, such as carrot or chocolate cake £2. Chai tea made fresh £2.20 and they have soya milk.

No alcohol allowed. There's a small garden where people can smoke.

Children welcome, high chairs and they plan to upgrade the toilets with nappy–changing facilities. Free wifi.

They have a small room downstairs with yoga and meditation classes, Reiki and massage.

Kalpna

Indian vegetarian restaurant

2–3 St Patrick Square, Edinburgh EH8 9EZ
Tel: 0131–667 9890
Open: Mon–Sat 12.00–14.00, 17.30–22.30, Sun closedl
May to Sept also open Sun 18.00–22.30
www.kalpnarestaurant.com

Gujarati and other dishes from North and South India, around 40% of which are vegan.

Lunch £7 buffet every day with 2 salads, 2 starters, 3 curries, 2 rice, bread, chutneys.

Dinner mains from £4.95, dosas around £10, thali £16.95, vegan thali £13.50. Rice £2.50–£5, brown rice available.

House wine £10.50 bottle, £2.50 glass. Well behaved children welcome, no high chairs. Visa, MC (£90 limit). Outside catering.

The Chocolate Tree

Vegetarian chocolate cafe & shop

123 Bruntsfield Place, Edinburgh EH10 4EQ
Tel: 0131-228 3144
Open: Mon–Sat 08.00-20.00
Sun 9.00-20.00
www.the-chocolate-tree.co.uk
Facebook: The Chocolate Tree

Come here for dessert! There's nothing savoury, it's all sweet stuff, all vegetarian, and they get lots of vegans although many things that might be vegan elsewhere aren't here, but what is is gorgeous. Mostly organic which means a lot is fairly traded though not necessarily certified as such. 26 seats inside, more outside in summer, but if it's packed you can grab take-away.

Among cakes, chocolate tarts £2.80–3.20 are a speciality, such as vegan chocolate hazelnut cake, which has a shortbread base covered with a rich layer of hazelnut chocolate, also a version with berries on top.

Ice-cream is dairy but they have fruit and chocolate sorbets (£2 one scoop, £3 two, £4 three) which have so much fruit or chocolate they taste like ice-

cream. Milkshakes £3 can be vegan if they use sorbet instead of ice-cream.

Eight kinds of hot drinking chocolate can all be served vegan, £2 blended organic origin, £2.80 single origin which has a more distinctive flavour (like with whisky), thick Spanish style £3. Flavours include Alpaco with jasmine and orange floral aromas, or light and fruity Madagascan.

Loose teas £2.20 pot for one. Artisan Roast Edinburgh coffee, latte, cappucino £1.80-2.20, luxury mocha £2.80. They have soya milk. Red espresso £2-2.50 is tea, latte or cappuccino made in the coffee machine but with caffeine-free Rooibos tea.

Also home-made lemonade, Fentimans and Belvoir soft drinks.

The chocolate shop has some yummy vegan ones such as mango and chili, raspberry and ginger, spearmint, Marmite, Thai spice, marzipan and strawberry, and at Christmas they do a vegan chocolate selection box. Dairy-free chocolate hazelnut spread. Cakes to order.

Children welcome, baby changing. Well behaved dogs welcome if they sit quietly under the table. MC, Visa.

The Auld Hoose

Omnivorous pub grub

23–25 St Leonard's St, Edinburgh, EH8 9QN.
Tel: 0131–668 2934
Food served Mon–Sat 12–21.30, Sun 12.30–20.00. Open until 02.45 during the festival season, with food served a bit later than usual.
www.theauldhoose.co.uk
Facebook: The Auld Hoose

A studenty real ale pub with a large, unpretentious menu that has plenty of veggie options. Expect to pay £5–10 for a filling meal.

Modular vegan breakfast available until 5pm, £5.95–£7.50 depending on how many options you choose.

Pakoras, spring rolls and onion rings around £2. Mains £6.75 such as veggie haggis with neeps and tatties; vegan sausage and mash; mushroom pie. Double falafel burger £7.50. They have vegan guacamole.

Raspberry sorbet £3.95.

Tea and coffee £1.60, though they no longer offer soya milk as the demand for hot drinks is low.

The jukebox is very punk, metal and rock. 10% student discount. 15% discount for everybody on Mondays. Free wifi. Not licensed for children.

Chop Chop

Omnivorous Chinese restaurant

248 Morrison Street, Edinburgh, EH3 8DT
Tel.: 0131–221 1155
Open: Every day: 12–14.00 & 17.30–22.00.

76 Commercial Street, Commercial Quay, Leith, Edinburgh, EH6 6LX
Tel: 0131–553 1818
Open: Every day: 17.30–22.00 (not lunch)
www.chop–chop.co.uk

These two new Chinese places pride themselves on fresh food, with noodles and dumplings made on site. They're great places to take a large group and have loads of veggie options. They've got a brilliant loyalty scheme in which you get points for every pound you or a friend mentioning your name spends, that can be cashed in for vouchers. You also get vouchers on your birthday.

Portion of 8 vegetable dumplings £4.10; hot and sour soup £2.95; noodles in sweet and sour sauce £6.75; large beancurd salad with sesame oil, spring onion and coriander £9.10; small cucumber and garlic salad £3.85.

Desserts include apple in caramelised sugar £6.90; and peanut butter, sesame and raisin dumplings £3.55.

Large range of fruit juices and fizzy drinks aroud £1.50–2.00; Chinese and other beers £1.80–£3.55. Chinese tea per table of 4 £1.60. Large wine list.

Business lunch special £7.50.

Small and large options available for almost everything. They bring the food as it is cooked, to encourage each table to share.

Vegan options list available.

Children welcome, high chairs and child–sized portions.

Earthy Market Cafe
Southside, Ratcliffe Terrace
Omnivorous organic cafe-deli & shop

In Earthy Food Market, 33–41 Ratcliffe Terrace
(a continuation of Causewayside), **Southside**,
Edinburgh EH9 1SX
Tel: 0131–667 2967
Shop: Mon–Fri 9.00–19.00, Sat 9.00–18.00,
Sun 10.00–18.00
Cafe: Mon–Fri 9.00–18.00, Sat 9.00–17.00,
Sun 10.00–17.00
www.earthy.co.uk
Facebook: Earthy Foods & Goods

One of two organic shops, this central
one has a cafe-deli plus lots of food to
grab and run from the fridge. This
branch has books, alcohol and a
freezer. Note there is also a meat
counter. For more on what the shop
sells, see the Shops section below.

The large cafe and deli counter is 50%
vegetarian with a lot of cheese and
some vegan choices, tofu, falafel etc.
Sandwiches, soup, daily tarts and hot
specials, such as vegan smokey
auberine, dill and cashew nut tart, or
squash, fresh corn, chilli and coriander
fritters.

The fridges have 8 or 10 kinds of grab-
and-go salad boxes which are always
vegetarian and mostly vegan, £4.95
regular, £6.95 large, such as (these are
all vegan) caraway, coriander and
coconut couscous; dark lentils, bulgar
wheat, chilli and pistachio; sesame, soy,
chilli, coriander soba noodle salad; char
grilled aubergines with spciy tomato
sauce; kohlrabi, carrot, cranberry and
dill coleslaw.

Home-made cakes £2.95 eat in, £2.50
take-away such as egg-free chocolate
cake. Organic Fairtrade hot drinks
£2.25; they have Bonsoy soya milk.

Children very welcome, high chairs.
Outside seating, dogs welcome and
they can provide water.

Customer car park. Also an online wine
store by the case which shows which are
vegan. Customer car park. MC, Visa.

Edinburgh Larder
Omnivorous cafe and deli

15 Blackfriars Street, Edinburgh, EH1 1NB
Tel: 0131–556 6922
Open: Mon to Sat 08.00–17.00, Sun 09.00–
17.00
www.edinburghlarder.co.uk

A new cafe with an attached deli shop
selling a range of specialist foodie gifts,
such as jams and unusual teas. The cafe
has a vegan–friendly menu with options
clearly marked. It's light and airy, with
artwork on the walls.

Breakfast options (served till midday)
include veggie haggis on toast, and
granola with soya milk, both £4.50.

Salad and bread deli plate with options
like olive tapenade £4.95. Hummus and
roast pepper sandwich £4.95.

Lots of cakes and biscuits, £2–2.95,
including gluten-free. Vegan options
include the very popular lemon and
almond polenta cake.

Range of teas and coffees £1.50–2.50.
Juices and smoothies around £3. Local
ales £2.50–3.50. Their elderflower
cordial (£1.50) is made with fresh
flowers picked themselves.

Children's menu.

The Elephant House

Omnivorous cafe

21 George IV Bridge, Edinburgh EH1 1EN
Tel: 0131–220 5355
Open: (Oct–Apr) Sun–Thurs 08.00–21.00,
Fri–Sat 08.00–22.00. In summer months
open until 23.00 every day.
www.elephanthouse.biz

An award-winning coffee house full of
elephants of all shapes and sizes that's
popular with students, writers and
anybody wanting to relax. A number of
novelists frequent the place. The menu
is around half vegetarian and focuses on
light meals for around £4–6, with
options such as mixed olives; elephant
veggie burger £5.50; tortillas with
hummus and salsa; baked potato with
veggie chilli; and Asian spinach salad.
They have vegan and gluten–free cakes
for £3.25 such as carrot cake; and apple
pie.
Pot of tea for one £1.95; for two £2.95.
Coffee ranges from £1.70 for a filter
coffee to £2.60 for a large cappuccino.
Good selection of wines, ales, whiskies
and cider.
Children welcome, high chairs.

Filmhouse Cafe–Bar

Omnivorous cafe in cinema

88 Lothian Road, Edinburgh EH3 9BZ
Tel: 0131–229 5932
Open: Sun–Thu 10.00–23.30,
Fri–Sat 10.00–00.30. Food served 10–22.00
with breakfast menu 10.00–12.00
www.filmhousecinema.com/cafe–bar

A large, busy cafe in a popular independent cinema. The menu is about half
vegetarian and they always have vegan
options such as hummous with mixed
leaves and pita bread; falafel; mixed
salad bowl; baked potatoes £4.95. Daily
special £7 upwards. Soup (always
vegan) with a bread roll £3.50.
Dishes tend to come with butter
portions unless you state otherwise.
Children welcome till 8pm, 3 high
chairs. Free wifi. "Food for a Fiver" offer
3–5pm. MC, Visa.

Los Cardos

Mexican omnivorous cafe

281 Leith Walk, Edinburgh EH6 8PD
Tel: 0131 555 6619
Open: Sun–Thu 12.00–21.00,
Fri–Sat: 12.00–22.00
www.loscardos.co.uk

A new burrito takeaway with some tables, half way along Leith Walk. The small menu features rice and pinto or black beans in a burrito with a choice of fillings, such as fried peppers and onions, dairy-free guacamole, lettuce and salsa. The food is made up to order, so it's easy to adapt dishes. Expect to pay £5–6 for a burrito.

Piemaker

Omnivorous pie and pasty takeaway

38 South Bridge, Edinburgh EH1 1LL
Tel: 0757 276 7718
Open: Mon–Wed 09.00–20.00,
Thu 09.00–23.00, Fri 09.00–01.00,
Sat 10.00–01.00, Sun 10.30–23.00

There's plenty for veggies in this long-established Edinburgh institution. It's not far from Royal Mile and near the studenty area of Southside.

Typically 9 meatless savoury pies, with 4 vegan such as Moroccan veg; Mexican veg; Thai mushroom and pepper; and balti curry. Vegan options are clearly marked on the big wall menu and very good value at £1.85. Sweet pies are the same price and include apple; apple and raspberry; and maple and pecan nut. You won't find cheaper hot stodge in town and this place is justifiably popular.

Union of Genius

Omnivorous soup cafe

8 Forrest Road, Edinburgh EH1 2QN
Tel: 0131-226 4436
Open: Mon-Fri: 10:00-15:00, Sat-Sun closed
Planning to open for breakfast and Saturdays
in 2012
www.unionofgenius.com
www.facebook.com/UnionOfGenius
Twitter: UnionofGenius

Scotland's first soup cafe opened
October 2011. They use locally-sourced
ingredients, flavour-matched with
artisan breads from Edinburgh's bakers.
Always vegetarian and vegan soups and
vegan and gluten-free cakes. Follow
them on Facebook or Twitter for today's
soup menu.

Typically there will be two veggie and
two vegan soups £3.50 (eat in or take-
away), £4.50 large (pint), with two slices
of bread. Vegan soups include pumpkin
with black onion seed and sumac;
tagine spiced chickpea; carrot,
butternut squash and coconut; minestrone.

They opened with all-vegan gluten-free
cakes £2 such as banana and walnut,
pumpkin and goji berry. Also
Montezuma chocolate which includes
vegan, and vegetable crisps.

Belu water, soft drinks, James White
organic apple juice, ginger beer, Whole
Earth cans, 70p-£1.60. Brewhaha local
Glasgow tea £1.50 standard or large.
Artisan Roast coffee from £1.80 to
£2.20 for a large latte, they will get soya
milk if there's demand.

Free wifi. Books to read. Children
welcome. Dogs welcome.

All take-away packaging and cutlery is
made from compostable plant starches,
which you bring back for them to
compost so it doesn't end up in landfill,
and give you loyalty points too towards
free coffee.

Cash only at the moment, cashpoint
nearby.

Edinburgh Indian

Kismot

Indian omnivorous restaurant

29 St Leonards Street, Edinburgh, EH8 9QN,
Tel: 0131-667 0123
Open: Every day 16.30-23.30
www.kismot.co.uk

Very popular Indian restaurant with a
huge menu. Vegetarian starters £2-3
include pakoras; samosas; and chickpea
puri with puffed bread. Curries start at
£8 and include Afghan chickpea, lemon
and ginger; spinach with tomatoes; hot
and sour balti; and baby aubergines
with potatoes in tomato and onion
sauce. The "Kismot Killer" costs £4 extra
and is described as "The hottest curry in
Scotland." Any diner who finishes it gets
a refund and their photo earns a place in
their Hall of Fame. Those who don't
manage are consigned to the Hall of
Shame. You have to sign a disclaimer
before eating! At the time of going to
print, nobody has managed the vegetarian version.

Boiled rice £2.85. Chips £2.

Range of fruit juices £1.85. Tea £2.50.
Not licenced, though you can bring your
own booze and there's no corkage.
Children welcome. All cards accepted.

Mosque Kitchen

Omnivorous Indian & Pakistani restaurant

31–33 Nicolson St. Edinburgh EH8 9BX
Tel: 0131-667 4035
Open: Every day 11.30–22.30 (closed Friday 13.00–13.45, for prayers)
www.mosquekitchen.co.uk

A good place to get a curry, that's around half vegetarian. The veggie options are potato and lentil-based curries cooked in vegetable oil rather than ghee, that come in generous portions, with rice and/or bread. £12 including drinks for a buffet. But you can eat for £3-5 such as rice and lentils. Children welcome, high chairs. No dogs. Cash only.

Suruchi

Indian omnivorous restaurant

14A Nicholson St, Edinburgh EH8 9DB
Tel: 0131-556 6583
Open: Every day 11.00–14.00 & 17.00–23.00
www.suruchirestaurant.com

Food from all over India, cooked by Indian chefs. The menu is informative about the origins of dishes and a lot more inventive and interesting than similar local restaurants, with options like veggie haggis gram flour fritters for £4.50. Around 30% of the food is vegetarian and you can get two courses and a drink for under £20 per person. Typical starters include vegetable pakora £3.50; samosas with coriander chutney £4.50; and chickpea, potato and banana chaat £4.50.
Typical main courses include chana (chickpea) masala £8.50; aubergines pan-fried with chillis and ginger £8.50; and potato koftas £8.95.
House wine £10-12 bottle, £2.50 glass. Children welcome, high chairs. 10% discount to Vegan Society members. MC, Visa. Another branch in Leith at 121 Constitution Street EH6 7AE. Tel: 0131-554 3268.

Tanjore

South Indian omnivorous restaurant

6–8 Clerk Street, Edinburgh EH8 9HX
Tel: 0131-478 6518
Open: Mon–Fri 12.00–14.30 (later if busy), 17.00–22.00; Sat– Sun 17.00–22.00
www.facebook.com/pages/
Tanjore/208115122566139

Big vegetarian selection of dosas (stuffed rice pancakes), idlies (rice cakes), vadais (lentil doughnuts) and uttapam (lentil pizza). Ghee isn't used, so the vegetarian options are almost all vegan. Selection of 6 bhajis and other starters £3-4. Mains £5.50-7.50. 6 types of vegetable curry. Thalis. Monster family dosa.
For dessert you can have banana dosa with nuts and jaggery sugar £4.
Coffee and tea £1-2. They don't have soya milk. No alcohol, but you can bring your own. Children welcome. MC, Visa.

Edinburgh Italian

Pizza Express, Edinburgh

Omni pizza restaurant & take-away

1 **Deanhaugh Street, Stockbridge** EH4 1LU
Tel: 0131–332 7229
Open: Mon–Sun 11.30–22.30, Fri–Sat 23.00

32 **Queensferry St, West End** EH2 4QS
Tel: 0131–225 8863
Open: Mon–Sun 11.30–22.30, Fri–Sat 23.00

Victoria Terrace, 59/63 **George IV Bridge**,
Edinburgh EH1 1RN
Tel: 0131–225 9669
Open: Mon–Sun 11.30–23.00, Fri–Sat 24.00

23 **Northbridge**, Edinburgh EH1 1SB (between
Newtown and old town, near the Royal Mile)
Tel: 0131–557 6411
Open: Mon–Sun 11.30–23.00, Fri–Sat 24.00

111 **Holyrood** Road, Edinburgh EH8 8AU (at
the bottom of the Royal Mile, 2 mins from
Holyrood Palace and the Scottish Parliament)
Tel: 0131–557 5734
Open: Mon–Sun 11.30–22.00, Fri–Sat 22.30

2a, 2nd Floor, **Ocean Terminal** Shopping
Centre, Edinburgh EH6 6JJ
Tel: 0131–555 0606
Open: Mon–Sun 11.30–22.30, Fri–Sat 23.00

Waterview House, **Leith**, Edinburgh EH6 6QU
Tel: 0131–554 4332
Open: Mon–Sun 11.30–22.30, Fri–Sat 23.00

2 McArthur Glen designer outlet village,
Livingston, West Lothian EH54 6QP
Tel: 01506–417 543
Open: Sun–Thu 11.30–22.00, Fri–Sat 23.00
www.pizzaexpress.com for menus and
ingredient lists with vegan suitability

See Glasgow section for menus.

Edinburgh Japanese

Wagamama, Edinburgh

Omnivorous Japanese restaurant

1 Castle Terrace (corner of Lothian Road),
Edinburgh EH1 2DP
Tel: 0131–229 5506
Open: Mon–Sat 11.00–23.00,
Sun 12.30–22.00
www.wagamama.com

Huge new restaurant with 130 seats
opened 2nd November 2011 after a
Facebook campaign by hundreds of
fans. For menus see Glasgow section.

Empires

Omnivorous Turkish restaurant

24 St Mary's St, Edinburgh, EH1 1SU
Tel: 0131– 466 0100
Open: Mon–Thu 17.00–23.00,
Fri–Sun 12.00–23.00
www.empirescafe.wordpress.com

This Turkish restaurant has a large menu of meze dishes for £3.95 and offers a good range of veggie options, such as marinated artichoke hearts; stuffed vine leaves and okra in tomato, onion and pepper sauce; and walnuts in olive oil with lemon and spices. You can build a colourful banquet filled with flavours and textures for around £12 a head. A few main meals also, but with limited meat–free choice.

Not licenced, bring your own for a small corkage charge. Fizzy drinks £1.95. Booking recommended, especially at weekends when they have live acoustic music. Children welcome, though they don't have high chairs. Cash and cheque only.

Hanam's

Omnivorous Kurdish restaurant

3 Johnston Terrace, Edinburgh, EH1 2PW
(right next to the castle)
Tel: 0131–225 1329
Open: Every day, 12.00 – late
www.hanams.com

This authentic halal Kurdish place has a large range of starters for around £4.50 that include hummus; tabbouleh; fatoush; and baba ghanoush. Olive platter £3. Mains cost around £9 and include Kurdish vegetable kebab; and okra or aubergine with tomatoes and garlic. Rose or mango sorbets £3.50.

Teas coffees and juices are all around £2. Large range of non–alcoholic wines and beers. Bring your own booze for no corkage.

Children welcome and they have high chairs. Balcony and some outside seating. All cards accepted.

Earthy Food Market
Southside, Ratcliffe Terrace

Omnivorous organic shop & cafe–deli

33–41 Ratcliffe Terrace (a continuation of Causewayside) EH9 1SX
Tel: 0131–667 2967
Shop: Mon–Fri 9.00–19.00, Sat 9.00–18.00, Sun 10.00–18.00
Cafe: Mon–Fri 9.00–18.00, Sat 9.00–17.00, Sun 10.00–17.00
www.earthy.co.uk
Facebook: Earthy Foods & Goods

One of two shops, this is the central one which also has a cafe/deli plus lots of food to grab and run from the fridge. This branch also has books, alcohol and a freezer. Note there is also a meat counter.

In both shops, you'll find lots of organic or local fruit and veg. Bread, rolls and focaccia by James the Baker, Dough Remi, Au Gourmand. Clearspring Japanese foods. Scottish pickles and chutneys, oatcakes.

They're not big on vegan cheeses or meat substitutes but do have the new Redwood mince, Cauldron sausages, and Engine Shed local soya milk, tofu including smoked and marinaded, and tofu burgers. Vegan chocolate by Booja Booja, Montezuma, Organica.

Bodycare brands include Faith in Nature, Suma, Natracare and Organyc C.

Beaming Baby nappies and bodycare. Baby food by Baby Zili, Organix, and Plum food.

Cleaning products by BioD, Ecover, Attitude, Ecoleaf and Ecoforce.

The Southside **Earthy Market Cafe, which closes one hour before the shop,** is a large cafe and deli counter. It's 50% vegetarian with a lot of cheese and some vegan choices, plus lots of vegan salads to grab and go in the fridges. For more on the cafe, see the omnivorous restaurants section above.

The Southside branch also sells alcohol with Vintage Roots wines, local cider, Heather ales, Broughton Ales, Black Isle Brewery, Caledonian Brewery, organic spirits.

Customer car park. Also an online wine store by the case which shows which are vegan. MC, Visa.

Earthy Food Market
Portobello

Omnivorous organic shop

19–21 Windsor Place, Portobello, EH15 2AJ (just off Portobello High Street)
Open: Mon–Fri 9.00–18.00, Sat 10.00–17.00, Sun 10.00–17.00
Tel: 0131–344 7930
www.earthy.co.uk
Facebook: Earthy Foods & Goods

This second branch opened August 2011 in Portobello, Edinburgh's trendy seaside area, 15 minutes by bus from the centre of the city. Portobello has a good arts scene, an organic market the first Saturday of the month, some organic cafes, and you can enjoy a nice walk on the beach.

The range of products is very similar to the Southside store, but being outside the centre there is more room for larger versions of pre–packed items such as grains and oils. They don't sell alcohol or have a freezer. A deli (but no seating) was due to be added as this book went to press. They have applied for a licence to sell alcohol, and will be doing Ecover refills and books.

Edinburgh Centre of Nutrition & Therapy

Health shop & complementary clinic

11 Home Street, Edinburgh EH3 9JR (at the road junction of Tollcross, a couple of minutes' walk from Princes Street)
Tel: 0131-229 1077
Shop: Mon–Sat 10.00–18.00
Therapies Mon–Sat 9.00–21.00
Closed Sun
www.ecnt.co.uk

This place is very popular with guests at local B&Bs. They don't sell food but do have lots of nice things to pamper yourself with, plus treatments.

Therapies include GP doctor, nutrition MOT, physiotherapy, Human Givens, psychotherapy, craniosacral, Bowen, chiropractic, life coaching, Emotional Freedom Technique, Bach Flower, Reiki, homeopathy, pilates. Massage includes Indian head, sport and remedial, hot stones, Thai foot, Indonesian, Chinese, therapeutic, Swedish, Oriental body balance, aromatherapy, reflexology.

The shop has Absolute Aromas essential oils full range and carrier oils, massage waxes, natural soaps, bath salts, hair care and cosmetics gift sets, hand-made cards, candles, gift wrapped baskets. Lots of nutrition and health books. Supplements by Solgar, Higher Nature, Biocare, Nutri, Vogel/Bioforce, Pukka, Nature's Plus and others. MC, Visa.

Hanover Healthfoods

Health food shop

40 Hanover St, Edinburgh EH2 2DR
Tel: 0131-225 4291
Open: Mon–Sat 9.30–17.30, Thu till 18.30, Sun closed
www.hanoverhealth.co.uk
Facebook: Hanover Healthfoods

Edinburgh's first health food shop opened here in 1904, probably the oldest health food store in the world. Offers personal advice from well trained staff as well as stocking a wide range of health foods and vitamins; the staff have 70 years' experience between them.

They don't do chilled and frozen foods (they say go to Holland & Barrett round the corner), the fridge has cold drinks. Lots of snacks and sweets, oatcakes, vegan chocolate by Plamil and sometimes others.

Bodycare includes Dr Hauschka, Weleda, Barefoot Botanicals, Green People and Lavera, Faith in Nature, Natracare. Supplements and herbal rememedies by Solgar, Higher Nature, Pharmanord, Nature's Aid, Quest, Lamberts, Biocare, Nutri, Viridian, Pukka, sports nutrition. Weleda homeopathy. Absolute Aromas essential oils. Monthly allergy testing.

Postal service available. MC, Visa.

Henderson's Shop

Vegetarian cafe and food shop with take-away counter

92 Hanover Street, Edinburgh EH2 1DR
Tel: 0131–225 6694
Open: Mon–Fri: 08.00–19.00,
Sat 10.00–18.00, Sun 10.00–16.00
www.hendersonsofedinburgh.co.uk/deli.php

Long-established (since 1962) health food shop above their restaurant and next door to their bistro. Local and organic produce including tea, coffee, fruit and bread from their bakery next door. Nuts and dried fruit, but not grains and pulses. Gluten-free products.

Fridge with drinks, take-away salads, pasties, sandwiches, rolls, panini, hummus, tofu, soya yogurt. Smoothies from the restaurant downstairs. No freezer.

Vegan chocolate such as Lazy Days, Booja Booja, Plamil, Divine, Montezuma. Organic vegan beer and wine. Vegetarian and vegan hampers. Eco-friendly and fairly-traded gifts.

They don't sell bodycare or supplements. MC, Visa, Amex.

The deli counter has hot and cold food with lots of organic, gluten-free and vegan options. Sandwiches, soups, pies, smoothies, juices and hot drinks to take away.

For more about the cafe area, see their entry in the vegetarian restaurants.

Jan de Vries, Edinburgh

Health food shop & complementary therapies clinic

39 Newington Road, Edinburgh EH9 1QW
Tel: 0131–662 0250
Open: Mon–Sat 9.00–17.30, Sun closed
www.jandevrieshealth.co.uk

Health foods, supplements and vitamins. Local organic bread. No fridge or freezer, but they have take-away meals ready to eat such as couscous and beans, pasta and veg, three beans and sweetcorn. Vegan chocolate by Naked, Raw Health, Plamil, cacao nibs, Noble Choice, Booja Booja.

Bodycare by Barefoot Botanicals, full range Weleda, Dead Sea Spa Magik, Avalon, Jason, Dr Bronner, Natracare, Weleda Baby.

Supplements by Bioforce, Nature's Aid, Solgar, Pharmanord, all of Floradix, Weleda homeopathy, Jan de Vries flower remedies and lots more. Tisserand and Julia Lawson essential oils.

Cleaning by Ecover and refills, Method. Books.

Therapy rooms and therapists: chiropody, podiatry, nutritional adviser and weight management programme, acupuncture and Reiki, osteopath, NLP, herbalist, Swedish and deep tissue and Hawaiian massage, life coach, bach flower, gem lamp therapy, allergy testing. Jan de Vries himself is in the shop 2 days a month for consultations. MC, Visa.

Jordan Valley Wholefoods

Omnivorous world food shop & deli

8 Nicolson Street, Edinburgh EH8 9DJ
013– 557 5534
Open: Mon–Sat 10.00–19.00,
Sun 12.00–18.00

Stock up for a picnic or midnight feast in this fabulous mostly vegetarian shop, with veggie and vegan foods clearly marked. They make their own range of vegetarian and vegan patés, pies, dips and pastries, including vegan cakes. Look out for these in other shops all over Edinburgh.

Wholefoods, grains, beans, fruits. Food from Turkey, Japan, Nepal, Morocco and China. Lots of spices. But the best bit is the fridges with dips such as hummus and baba ghanoush, veggie patés, pasties, sausage rolls, hempseed falafel. There is lots of Mediterranean, with olives, dolmades, stuffed aubergines and peppers. Take-away sandwiches, pastries, pies, slices of cakes, flapjacks, Turkish delight and falafels.

Every Tuesday from 6pm tasting nights with tea and samples. Downstairs cafe on the way, opening 2012. Outside catering. MC, Visa.

Cakes, pies, sauces and dips from their factory in Fife are also on sale at Real Foods, Margiottas and other shops here and in Glasgow.

Lush, Edinburgh

Cruelty-free cosmetics

44 Princes Street, Edinburgh EH2 2BY
Tel: 0131-557 3177
Open: Mon– Sun 10.00–18.00
www.lush.co.uk

Fun things for back at your guesthouse such as fizzing bath balls and chocolate soap. Most products are vegan and labelled so.

The New Leaf

Vegetarian organic wholefood shop

23 Argyle Place, Marchmont,
Edinburgh EH9 1JJ
Tel: 0131–228 8840
Open: Mon–Sat 9.30–18.00, Sun closed
www.newleafedinburgh.com

Everything is vegetarian and most organic (they are Soil Association members) with lots of Fairtrade and local.

Organic fruit and veg. Local bread. Fridge and freezer with lots of vegan things such as cheeses, Redwood sausage and "bacon", local hummus and organic tofu, Swedish Glace vegan ice-cream. Local vegan pasties delivered Wednesday, should have them till Saturday. Vegan chocolate by Plamil, Organica, Montezuma, Booja Booja.

Bodycare by Faith in Nature, Weleda, Suma, Lavera, Caurnie Scottish soap and shampoo, Natracare, Green People children's bath stuff.

Cleaning products with an astonishing 20 refills for Ecover, Ecoleaf and BioD, plus Caurnie shampoo and Faith in Nature lavender hand soap.

Children's play corner. 10% discount on whole cases. Student discount. MC, Visa.

Real Foods

Vegetarian wholefood supermarket

37 Broughton Street, Edinburgh EH1 3JU
Tel: 0131–557 1911
Open: Mon–Fri 08.00–20.00,
Sat 9.00–18.30, Sun 10.00–18.00

8 Brougham St, Tollcross, Edinburgh EH3 9JH
Tel: 0131–228 1657
Open: Mon–Fri 8.00–18.30, Sat 9.00–18.00,
Sun 10.00–17.00
www.realfoods.co.uk

Huge, well-stocked shops with stuff you won't find elsewhere and long opening hours. Thousands of vegan products. Lots of organic fruit and veg. Plenty of bread including gluten-free. Fridge with take-away sandwiches, wraps, rolls, pasties, sushi, hummus, tofu, vegan cheeses, meat substitutes. Freezers with ready meals, Swedish Glace, Booja Booja and other vegan ice-cream and desserts.Vegan chocolate by Plamil, Montezuma, Divine, Organica, Willie's, Booja Booja.

80 organic and vegan wines, some beer. At least 2,000 bodycare products by Faith in Nature, Jason, Lavera, Green People, Urtekram, Weleda, Essential Care, Natracare. Maltex and other nappies.

Supplements include the full range of Solgar, Viridian, Bioforce, Quest, Biocare, Nature's Plus, Nature's Aid, Higher Nature and lots more. Some Weleda and New Era homeopathy, Nelson's Bach Flower. Aqua Oleum and Absolute Aromas essential oils. Occasionally visiting practitioners doing evening events and late night shopping, see the webshop where you can buy tickets.

Cleaning products by Ecover, Almawin, Attitude, Suma Ecoleaf with refills if you ask. Health and diet books, incense, cards.

Early Bird discount scheme, just go early and sign up for 10% off 8–10am Mon–Fri, Sat 9–10am, Sun 10–11am. Over 250 items on special offer every month, and look out for half-price daily manager's specials.

Huge online shop with vegan clearly marked, thousands of items for immediate delivery. MC, Visa.

Valvona and Crolla

Italian Delicatessen

19 Elm Row, Edinburgh EH7 4AA (off Leith Walk)
Tel: 0131–556 6066
Open: Mon–Thu: 8.30–18.00,
Fri–Sat 8.00–18.30, Sun 10.30–16.00
www.valvonacrolla.co.uk

Classy Italian deli which stocks a wide range of bread, vegetables, dark chocolate and Mediterranean staples such as sun-dried tomatoes, grilled aubergines, and olives. Roasted vegetable sandwich £2.75.
There's now also a cafe/bar though it has little for vegetarians.

Holland & Barrett

Health food shops

Unit 3 Hanover Building, **Rose St** EH2 2NN
Tel: 0131–226 5802
Open: Mon–Sat 9.00–18.00,
Sun 11.00–17.00

---

10 **Shandwick Place**, Edinburgh EH2 4RN
Tel: 0131–226 6138
Open: Mon–Sat 08.00–18.00,
Sun 11.30–16.30

---

124 **Nicolson Street**, Edinburgh EH8 9EH
Tel: 0131–667 2921
Open: Mon–Sat 9.00–18.00, Sun 12–17.00

Unit 31 **Cameron Toll** Shopping Centre, Lady Road, Edinburgh EH16 5PB
Tel: 0131–664 5987
Open: Mon–Wed 9.00–18.00, Thu 20.00, Fri 19.00, Sat 9.00–18.00, Sun 10.00–17.00

Unit RU27B **Ocean Terminal**, 98 Ocean Drive, Edinburgh EH6 6JJ
Tel: 0131–554 1302
Open: Mon–Fri 10.00–20.00,
Sat 10.00–19.00, Sun 11.00–18.00

---

7 Almond Vale South, **Livingston**, West Lothian EH54 6NB (just west of Edinburgh)
Tel:01506–430 021
Open: Mon–Sat 9.00–17.30, Thu 19.00,
Sun 10.30–17.00
hollandandbarrett.com

National chain of health food shops that sell bagged dried foods, supplements and vitamins. Lots of muesli, nuts, dried fruit, flapjacks and sweets. All Edinburgh branches have a fridge and freezer, and the first two in the city centre are good to grab lunch on the run such as vegetarian sausage rolls, pies, pasties and Jamaican patties.

Cruelty Free Edinburgh

Online resource

www.crueltyfree.org.uk/edinburgh

This website gives local news and views about where to eat out and shop vegan in the city.

Edinburgh Raw Food

Social group

www.meetup.com/Edinburgh-Raw-Foodies

Vegan raw food potluck meals, workshops and outings.

Edinburgh Vegans

Online resource

http://groups.yahoo.com/group/edveg
David Harrington 0789 686491
Mail@davidharrington.org.uk

Local branch of both UK Vegetarian and Vegan Societies.

Ethical Voice for Animals – Bunny Huggers

Animal rights campaigning group

54 Manor Place, Edinburgh, EH3 7EH
EVA stall 1pm every Saturday 1pm, weather permitting, opposite Balmoral Hotel, Edinburgh
www.ethicalvoiceforanimals.org.uk
info@ethicalvoiceforanimals.org.uk
Facebook: EVA For Animal Rights

National group set up in 2007, based in Edinburgh, working to end all forms of animal abuse. Lots of actions in Aberdeen, Dundee, Edinburgh, Glasgow, Inverness. Stalls, protests, demos, school talks, workshops, food fairs, film nights, fortnightly email newsletter, campaigning skills workshops.

Onekind

Animal rights campaigning group

10 Queensferry Street, Edinburgh EH2 4PG
Tel: 0131–225 6039
www.onekind.org

Formerly known as Advocates for Animals, this group focus on getting to the root of animal exploitation by raising the status of animals in society, rather than simply highlighting areas of animal abuse, and campaigning for changes in the law.
Runs glossy "We're not that different" advertising campaign, endorsed by celebrities.

Scotland for Animals

Online resource

www.scotlandforanimals.org

This website gives info about animal welfare campaigns and issues.

Vegan Edinburgh + Glasgow

Online resource

Facebook: Vegan Edinburgh + Glasgow
www.facebook.com/groups/106588816094435

This is a group for vegans, and people thinking about becoming vegan, in the central belt of Scotland.

Edinburgh VisitScotland Information Centre

Tourist information centre

3 Princes Street, Edinburgh EH2 2QP
Tel: 0845 22 55 121
+44-131-625 8625 (outside UK)
Open: Sep-Jun Mon-Sat 9.00-17.00, Sun 10.00-17.00;
Jul-Aug Mon-Sat 9.00-19.00, Sun 10.00-19.00
www.edinburghdaysout.com

Expert advice, accommodation booking service, free literature, coach and walking tours, discounted passes, Scottish gifts and souvenirs.

SCOTLAND Edinburgh

Tourist information websites
www.glasgowguide.co.uk
www.seeglasgow.com
www.glasgow.gov.uk/en/AboutGlasgow/Touristattractions

Glasgow

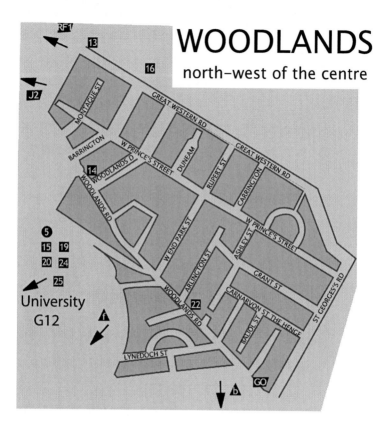

WOODLANDS
north–west of the centre

University
G12

▲ **Accommodation**
a Alamo Guest House
b Blue Sky Hostel
c Craigielea House B&B
d Alison Guest House
e Euro Hostel Glasgow
f Glasgow SYHA Hostel

■ **Shops**
GC Green City Wholefoods
GO Grassroots Organics
Holland & Barrett:
HB1 Queen Street
HB2 Sauchiehall Street
HB3 Gallowgate
IF Imrie Fruit, Thornaliebank
Jan de Vries:
J1 Shawlands
J2 West End
Lush:
L1 Buchanan Street
L2 Sauchiehall Street
QV Quality Vitamins & Herbs
Roots & Fruits:
RF1 West End
RF2 Argyle St
WF Whole Foods Market

Vegetarian Pubs & Restaurants

1   Mono
2   Stereo
3   Heavenly
4   Saramago at CCA
5   Tchai-Ovna
6   Tapa Bakehouse
13 The 13th Note
78 The 78

Omnivorous Restaurants

10 Assams
11 Banana Leaf S Side
12 Banana Leaf W End
13 Biblocafe
14 The Bay Tree
15 Falafel Petra
16 Grassroots Cafe
17 Green Chilli Cafe
18 Mr India's
19 The Left Bank
20 Little Italy
21 KoolBa
22 La Padella
23 Nanakusa
24 OATS Brasserie
25 OATS Cafe
    Pizza Express:
P1 Queen Street
P2 Sauchiehall Street
26 Tapa Coffeehouse
27 Wagamamam Central

Denistoun, G31

Kelvinhaugh, G3

Southside, G41

CENTRAL GLASGOW

Kelvingrove Accommodation

While there is as yet no vegetarian guest house in Glasgow that we know of, the following can provide a full breakfast for vegetarians and vegans.

Alamo Guest House

**Omnivorous guest house
and self-catering apartment**

46 Gray Street, Kelvingrove, Glasgow G3 7SE
Tel: 0141–339 2395
Underground: Kelvin Hall, Kelvin Bridge 5–10 mins walk
Train: Central & Queen Street 5 mins taxi
www.alamoguesthouse.com

A large Victorian house on a quiet street with views over a park. Each of the 12 rooms has its own look and character, from a luxury double with 3D tv to a small single. Prices range from £35 for a single room for multiple days during quiet weeks, to £52 during high season or when conferences are on nearby. Doubles £54–72, luxury room £105–155. Children under 4 free; for other ages check when booking.

Vegetarian breakfast options include a fruit salad with around 10 fruits including melon, mango, pineapple and grapes; 10 cereals; organic muesli; or a cooked breakfast of tomatoes, mushrooms, beans and toast. They have soya milk. High chairs. No smoking throughout. No pets. All cards accepted except Diners.

Each room has wifi, DVD player and there are over 400 DVDs.

Denistoun Accommodation

Alison Guest House

Omnivorous guest house

26 Circus Drive, Merchant City East, Glasgow G31 2JH
Tel: 0141–556 1431
Train: Alexander Parade (from Queen St) or Belgrove, bus 36, 38, 41 to centre
Open: all year
www.alisonguesthouse.co.uk

Despite the postcode, this guest house is only a mile from the centre of Glasgow and you can see the cathedral. The owner is an antiques dealer and the furnishings include Victorian pieces. 1 single from £27–30, 4 twin/double/family ensuite £23–27.50 per person. Variety of cooked and uncooked vegetarian choices, can cater for the occasional vegan. They have soya milk. Children of any age welcome. Pets welcome. Rooms have shaver point, tea/coffee making, tv and radio. Free wifi. MC, Visa.

Craigielea House B&B

Omnivorous bed and breakfast

35 Westercraigs, Glasgow G31 2HY
Tel: 0141–554 3446
Open: all year
smoothhound.co.uk/hotels/craigiel.html

Atmospheric early Victorian building in Denistoun, which is also only a mile from the city centre. Great value accommodation, 1 double and 2 twin rooms only £20–25 per person. Rooms have fridge, washbasin, wifi and TV. Breakfast can be brought to your room.

Breakfasts can be gluten-free or vegan with advance notice. Options include cereal, oatcakes, bean on toast, fruit salad and soya yoghurt. They have soya milk and are happy to buy things like vegan sausages in if you ask when booking.

Children over 8 welcome. No pets. Car park and on-street parking. Original artwork on walls and a sunny garden to sit in full of flowers. No credit cards.

Glasgow Hostels

Euro Hostel Glasgow

Omnivorous self-catering hostel

318 Clyde Street, Glasgow G1 4NR
Tel: 0141-222 2828
Open: all year, 24 hours
Central station 5 mins' walk
www.euro-hostels.co.uk

Clean and stylish looking hostel with self-catering facilities. Bar open to the public. All dorms and rooms ensuite.
Dorms for 4 to 14 £13-20, twin/double £18-26 per person, singles £29-40, family rooms with bunks £16-20, under-5 free, 15% student discount or if you become a fan on Facebook. Reduced rates for long stays.
Women only top floor with full length mirrors, hairdryers and extra hanging space, though it's not always available.
Continental breakfast included with toast, cereals, hot drinks, fruit; vegans should bring soya milk and spread, they have fridges in kitchen. Cook your own dinner in the guest kitchen and eat it in the tv lounge which has a pool table. Or go to the 13th Note and Mono veggie pubs 10 minutes walk away.
Quiet room for reading or playing cards. 24 hour reception. Tour bookings. Small souvenir shop. Tesco nearby. Luggage storage. Internet access £1 for 20 minutes, free wfi and skype when bar open 12.00-24.00. Wheelchair friendly building. Secure motorcycle parking and bicycle storage.

Blue Sky Hostel

Self-catering young adults only hostel

65 Berkeley Street, Charing Cross, Glasgow G3 7DX
Tel: 0141-221 1710
Open: all year, reception open 08.00-03.00
Train: Charing Cross
www.blueskyhostel.com

Calls itself the cheapest place to stay in Glasgow and ideal for a night out on the town being close to Sauciehall Street. Backpackers aged 18-35 only, no children. Around 50 beds £10.50, 4 to 14 in a dorm. Private double and triple £25-35. Lounge area beside self-catering kitchen with fridges. 2 internet terminals, no charge, free wifi. Free lockers. The 78 vegan pub and CCA Saramago vegan cafe are nearby MC, Visa.

Glasgow Youth Hostel

Self-catering SYHA family hostel with meals available

8 Park Terrace, West End, Glasgow G3 6BY
Tel: 0141-332 3004
Open: all year, 24 hours
Bus 44 from Buchanan bus station to Charing Cross. Underground: Kelvinbridge.
Train: Charing Cross
www.syha.org.uk

141 beds, architecturally impressive in two converted town houses with amazing wooden carved staircase. Within Kelvingrove Park with skate park and playground.
All rooms and dorms are ensuite. Dorms 4 to 8 people £15.50-25, doubles/twins £47-52, one single £25.50-35, family room for 4 £78-100. Cots and high chairs.
Continental cold breakfast £4.25, cooked £6.25 which they can tailor to vegans by discussion and you may get a discount, e.g. hash browns, beans,

tomatoes, toast, tea/coffee, juice, potato scones. Evening meals 18.00–20.30, 1 course £7, 2 £9.95, 3 £11.95; vegetarian option. The 78 vegan pub and Tchai-Ovna are nearby, and all the other veggie delights of Glasgow.

Kitchen and dining area for self-catering with pans, crockery, cookers, microwaves, shelving with some free stuff like tea, fridges and labels for marking your food. Lots of recycling. Sainsbury's nearby next to the bus stop, open 9.00–23.00.

TV lounge and pool table. 4 internet terminals 50p/half hour, wifi on ground floor. Leaflets and local magazines for what's on. Lockable bike shed. Conference room for 60 people. No lift as it's a listed building. No stag or hen parties. MC, Visa.

GLASGOW – veggie pub heaven

The 13th Note, page 42

Mono, page 46

The 78, page 44

Stereo, page 48

Heavenly, page 50

Saramago (CCA), page 52

The 13th Note

Independent music venue and bar with vegetarian cafe at one end. All food is vegan unless marked V for vegetarian if it contains dairy, which hase a separate preparation area.

Lunch till 5pm £4.50–4.95 includes tortilla wraps with salad and fillings such as falafel with beetroot tzatziki, "meetball", hummus, veg chilli; toasted wholemeal veggie bacon club sandwich; pizzas (can be without cheese for vegans).

Main menu all day until 10pm Starters and snacks £2–4.45 such as soup, bruschetta, nachos with salsa, mushroom paté with chilli jam and wholemeal toast, herby "meetball" with garlic bread, crispy tofu with mint and radish raita, house salad, Cajun spicy chips.

Mains £6.50–7.25 include veggie or falafel burger with salad and chips (extra toppings 95p such as hummus, hash browns, mushrooms, veggie bacon, coleslaw, chilli); sosage and spring onion mash with onion gravy; creamy coconut curry and rice; Pad Thai noodles and crispy tofu; haggis, neeps n tatties with creamy brandy peppercorn sauce; thali; super salad; mezze platter.

Saturday–Sunday full cooked brunch (12.00–17.00) £6.25 with sosage, veggie bacon, mushrooms, beans, hash brown, tattie scone, toast, tea or coffee. Scrambled tofu with truffle oil and fresh spinach on wholemeal toast £4.95. Tomato and chilli beans on toast £3.95.

Incredible desserts £2.70–4.50 are all vegan including cheesecake; ice-cream with optional liqueur; swally berries chocolate pot and strawberries in maple syrup and whiskey with shortbread; sticky toffee pudding. Toppings for any dessert 90p such as maple syrup, strawberry or fruits of the forest in sauce, chocolate sauce, toffee sauce.

Pot of tea £1.30. Cappuccino, latte, hot chocolate or mocha £1.60–£2. They have soya milk. Also flavoured soya milks, Ame and fruit juices.

50–60 King Street
Glasgow G1 5QT

Tel: 0141–553 1638

www.13thnote.co.uk
Facebook: The 13th Note

Open:
Mon–Sun 12.00–24.00,
food served until 22.00
approx

The Notecave venue space downstairs hosts gigs, comedy and private functions

Children welcome till 18.30; all gigs downstairs over–18

Non–vegan and gluten–free items marked on menu

All coffee and tea are Fairtrade

Alcohol includes vegan options. House wine £3.75 medium glass, £12.50 bottle.

Dogs welcome in the bar

Visa, MC

The 78

Opened in 2007 and great for vegan eating out or a relaxing drink. Previously the home of sister venue Stereo which has moved to the city centre, it is now revamped and re-decorated in a beautiful retro style, with a roaring coal fire, comfy armchairs, sofas, chunky wooden tables, floor length French windows and an old HMV 78 record player. The big menu includes generous main courses, daily specials, sandwiches and vegan desserts. This is the only one of Glasgow's venues where all the alcohol is vegan, and many also organic.

Weekend full cooked breakfast £7.50 with tempeh rashers, sausages, mushroom, beans, tomatoes, toast, fried potatoes or potato scone, tea or coffee.

Lunch menu includes soup with crusty bread £3.50; olives, garlic bread, side salad and chips all £2.50; wraps £4.50–4.95 such as VLT, falafel, or roast squash, butterbean and thyme hummus with crumbled garlic tofu.

Evening starters as above, plus coconut and bean chilli with tortilla chips £4.95; quinoa and millet cakes with beetroot glaze and salad £3.95; spring rolls or onion rings £2.50.

Mains £6.50–7.95 include curry of the day, falafel platter, tempeh burrito with all the trimmings, pie of the day, burger, chips with chips and salad (extra toppings available), and pumpkin seed and thyme crusted seitan with quinoa, roast squash steamed green and chilli sauce.

Desserts £3.95 include coconut and walnut chocolate torte with cream, and coffee and cinnamon infuseds dates with vanilla ice-crea and toasted almonds. Vegan ice-cream £1.50, 3 scoops £3.50, toppings 50p.

Mon–Fri all day specials The Daily Pot such as chilli, curry or stew £5, and Burger and Pint of Williams Bros lager £5.50.

Drinks Wine £3.95 glass, large 4.70, bottle 13.95. Bottled beers £2.50–4.40 include Samuel Smith's, Williams Bros, Black Isle, Weston's cider. Draft beers, stout and cider £2.50–4.20 pint. Coffee £1.90. Tea £1.60. Soya milk is the only milk they have.

Glasgow

Vegan pub & music venue

10-14 Kelvinhaugh Street
Glasgow G3 8NU

Tel: 0141-576 5018

www.the78cafebar.com
Facebook: The 78 Cafe Bar

Open:
Sun–Thu 12.30–24.00
Fri–Sat 12.00–24.00

Food serving times:
Lunch
Mon–Fri 12.30–17.00
Sat–Sun 12.00–17.00
Eve Mon–Sun 17.00–21.00

Meat Free Monday deal: two courses for £8 or 3 for £10

Tue: 25% student discount

Wed: open mic night

Thu from 5pm: the Dutchy Pot special menu with starters and desserts £2, mains £5. DJs 8pm playing reggae/dub

Weekends: free entertain-ment including dj's, live jazz Sun evening

Children welcome till 20.00
Children's portions

Dogs welcome at outside seating

All coffee and tea are Fairtrade

10% discount students and take-away

Visa, MC

Mono

Bar with a separate vegan cafe and a record shop Monorail Music, Good Press bookshop (small press and art) and gallery. Both cafe and bar have a relaxed atmosphere, with changing artwork and frequent live events. One customer says "Mono is my favourite because it's got everything, great selection of vegan beers which you can sup on an elevated platform, record shop with vinyl and CDs focusing on alternative/indie, and amazing cheesecake."

A selection of soft drinks are handcrafted on site using microbrewery vats. All wine and most beer is vegan and both vanilla and unsweetened soya milk are offered.

Starters and sides £1.95–3.95 such as soup, Thai potato cakes with spicy slaw, hummus and baba ghanoush with pitta, , cauliflower fritters with lime yogurt, spicy chips with aioli.

Sandwiches with side salad £4.95 such as bean burrito; falafel; smoked tofu, pesto mayo, tomato and spinach on toasted bread. Soup and sandwich £5.50.

Mains £7.50–7.95 vary with the seasons such as asparagus risotto, nasi goreng Indonesian spicy rice dish with various nuts, Portobello mushroom burger with chips, squash and spinach lasagne, couscous with roast veg.

Desserts around £4, such as chocolate and orange brownie with ice-cream, and cheesecake with summer berries or salt caramel sauce.

Meat-free Monday special offer two for one on main courses.

Brunch menu served on weekends. This changes weekly but includes breakfast burrito, pancakes with tempeh rashers and organic maple syrup, and scrambled tofu on toast.

Drinks House wine £13.95 bottle, £3.85 medium glass, £4.75 large. Organic lagers, ciders and bottled beers including Williams Brothers Brewery and Samuel Smith's.

Fairtrade teas, local roasted ethical coffee, soya latte, cappuccino £1.70–2.00. Homemade lemonades and ginger beer £1.50 half pint.

Vegan cafe and bar with record shop

12 King's Court
off King Street
Glasgow G1 5RB

Tel: 0141-553 2400

Train: High Street
or Argyle Street
Underground: St Enoch

www.monocafebar.com
Facebook: Mono Cafe Bar

www.monorailmusic.co.uk
Facebook: monorail music

Mon open:
Sun–Thu 11.00–24.00,
Fri–Sat 11.00–01.00

Food served 12.00–21.00

Monorail Music open:
Mon–Sat 11.00–19.00
Sun 12.00–19.00

Monday 2 for 1 on mains

Children welcome, high chairs

Outdoor summer seating, dogs welcome there

All wine and most beers vegan

MC, Visa

Stereo

Sister pub to Mono, this is a city centre late-opening cafe/bar, music venue and nightclub in a Mackintosh designed building. Everything is vegan except the option of cow's milk in hot drinks.

Flatbread sandwiches with side salad £4.50 such as baba ganoush, dates and mixed leaves on flatbread; VLT tempeh rashers with plum tomato, mayo and mixed leaves. Soup with bread £3.50. Soup and sandwich £5.50. Organic salads £5.50 with their homemade bread.

Tapas in three prices: £3.50 for patatas bravas, seared artichokes, grilled courgettes and pine nuts, hummus or baba ghanoush with flatbread, veg tempura with sweet chilli and soy dip, bruscheta, stuffed vine leaves with tahini dressing, herb potato cakes with chive aioli; £2.50 for chips, salad, garlic and herb flatbread, olives; £1.95 for curly kale crisps, mixed bean salad, green salad.

Mains £7.50-7.95 such as haggis fritters with chips and mushy peas; mezze platter; beetroot and pine nut tart with herb potato cakes; and various stonebaked pizzas, calzone and gnocchi. **Weekend brunch specials** till 5pm like burrito or a big breakfast with veggie sausage, tempeh rashers, beans, mushrooms, tomatoes and hash browns.

Desserts and cakes £1.50-3.50 change daily such as lemon drizzle, carrot or chocolate and chilli cake, banana and raspberry ice-cream sundae.

Meat-free Monday special offer e.g. 5 tapas for £10 all day.

Drinks Soft drinks £1.95-2.55 include Chegworth Valley organic juices, Fentimans, Whole Earth. Fairtrade teas or coffee £1.90, cappuccino and latte £1.90-2.40.

Some vegan beers, but not all as they're tied to a brewery. House wine medium glass £3.65, large £4.75, bottle £13.95.

Opposite is **The Old Hairdressers** run by the same people, a bar and gallery exhibition space, open 18.00-24.00, weekends 12.00-24.00, where the local Williams Brothers bottled and keg beer are vegan (June 2011 barnivore.com, but not cask conditioned beer though that is planned to change).

Glasgow

Vegan cafe/bar and music venue

22-28 Renfield Lane
Glasgow G2 5AR

Tel: 0141-222 2254

www.stereocafebar.com
Facebook: Stereo Cafe Bar

Open:
Sun-Wed 12.00-01.00,
Thu-Sat 12.00-03.00

Full menu until 21.00
Tapas until 24.00
Nightclub open to 3am

The basement is a live music venue

Children welcome until 8pm, high chairs

No dogs

MC, Visa

Heavenly

Heavenly is an independent vegan cafe/bar located in the heart of Glasgow. It serves a varied, full menu in addition to its daily specials. It has an independent music policy; creating a soothing atmosphere by day and an invigorating, toe-tapping feel for the late evening. Occasional DJs at weekends. Framed LP's on the wall.

Weekends till 6pm **breakfast** £7.45 with tempeh rashers, sausage, scrambled beech smoked tofu, roasted mushrooms, potato scone, grilled tomato, beans and toast.

Starters and snacks £2.95-3.45 such as soup of the day, tempura, polenta cakes with spinach and pesto, beatroot salad, crostini, hummus and pitta.

Wraps and sandwiches £4.25-4.50 include TLT tempeh rasher; falafel; grilled seitan; BBQ jackfruit.

Mains £5.95-7.95 include bangers and mash with red wine and onion gravy; kale Caesar salad with beech smoked tofu; sweet and sour tofu with rice; roast vegetable pie with creamy mash; marinated tofu burger with roasted peppers and mushrooms in an organic rolls, served with chips, onion rings and salad; Moroccan7-veg tagine stew with date and coconut couscous; daily specials.

All day lunch deal £4.95 soup and sandwich, sandwich and chips, or burger and beer.

Tuesday any two specials for £10.

Proper desserts £3.25-3.95 include sticky sponge with toffee sauce and ice-cream; apple and pear crumble with ice-cream or cinnamon custard; gingerbread with cinnamon custard.

Cakes: cupcakes and muffins, pastries, tarts all £1.95.

House wines are all vegan, as are most of the other drinks, and are marked if vegan. Bottle of wine £10.50, glass £2.95. Only Fosters isn't vegan, vegan beers include Heineken, Samuel Smith's, Becks, Brewdog Coffee, cappuccino, latte, hot choc (can be with mint or spices) £1.30-2.25. Teas £1.60. Irn Bru, juices, Whole Earth organic sodas, Fentimans, Red Bull, drinking vinegars £1.30-2.40.

Restaurant/cafe/bar with vegan food

185 Hope Street
Glasgow G2 2UL

Tel: 0141-353 0884

Open: Mon-Sun 12.00-24.00
Last food orders 20.00, but cakes all night

www.heavenlyglasgow.co.uk
Facebook Heavenly Cafe/Bar

All day lunch deal £4.95 soup and sandwich, sandwich and chips, or burger and beer.
Tuesday any two specials for £10.

Doggy bags if your eyes turn out to be larger than your stomach.

Kids welcome daytime, children's portions, 2 high chairs, baby changing

All wines vegan

No dogs

Free wifi

Occasional weekend DJs

Visa, MC

Saramago Cafe Bar (CCA)

Vegetarian cafe in arts centre, all food vegan

Centre for Contemporary Arts,
350 Sauchiehall St, Glasgow G2 3JD
Tel: 0141-332 7959
Reservations: 0141-352 4920
Open: Mon–Sat 10.00–24.00, Sun closed
Food served: 10.00–22.00
www.cca-glasgow.com/cafe

The arts centre cafe bar has had a re-vamp, with the entire menu now vegan apart from milk in hot drinks and alcohol such as Guinness.

Small plates £3.50 such as soup of the day; marinated aubergines; roast courgettes with pinenuts and raisins; roast pepper hummus or baba ghanoush with flatbread; patatas bravas; veg tempura with dip; spring rolls; dolmades with tahini dressing; bruschetta; artichoke hearts.

Flatbread sandwiches with salad £4.50 such as tofu sausage with mustard and onion; baba ghanoush and raisins; falafel; Mediterranean tapenade and plum tomatoes; Greek hummus and roast pepper. Soup and sandwich £5.50. Salads £5.95 such as roast butternut squash with lentils; Thai noodle with peppers and peanuts.

Main courses £7.50–7.95 such as ratatouille tart with salad; haggis fritters with chips and mushy peas; mezze platter; asparagus and broad bean risotto; various pasta; stonebaked pizza; calzone. Side dishes £2.50.

Desserts £3.95 are warm chocolate cake with cream or ice-cream, an amazing gelata affogato with amaretto liqueur and almond biscuits, and daily specials. Selection of ice-creams £3.50. 2-course lunch £6.50, 3-course £8.50. 2-course pre-theatre menu £8.95, 3-course £10.95.

Coffee, cappucino, latte £1.95–2.25, teas £1.60. They have soya milk. Vegan wine medium glass £3.85, large £4.75, bottle £13.95–18.95.

Bread baked on site each morning. Children welcome, high chairs. The upstairs bar section has outdoor terrace seating area, dogs welcome there. MC, Visa.

Tchai-Ovna House of Tea

Vegetarian cafe

42 Otago Lane, Glasgow G12 8PB
Tel: 0141-357 4524
Open: Every day 11.00-23.00
Underground: Kelvinbridge
www.tchaiovna.com

Chilled out teetotal tea shop and cafe with a range of vegetarian foods from around the world and over 80 types of unusual tea, sold by the bag and pot.

Starters/light meals £3.80 include soup or falafel in pita. Main meals £6.50 vary each day, typical options are red daal or curry with rice and salad. Sharing platter £10.50. Most of the food is vegan, including the cakes, which are all made on the premises with some unusual ones such as goji berry and raw chocolate £2.70.

Teas range from £2.20 to £5.50 for a half litre pot, depending on rarity. Fairtrade coffee £2.20. They have soya milk.

Gigs and storytelling at 8pm most evenings. Children welcome but no high chairs. Outdoor seating where you can smoke and bring a dog. Cash only.

Tapa Bakehouse

Vegetarian cafe, bakery & grocer

19-21 Whitehill St, Dennistoun (East End), Glasgow G31 2LH
Tel: 0141-554 9981
Open: Mon-Sat 08.00-18.00,
Sun 9.00-17.00
www.tapabakehouse.com

Glasgow's only certified organic bakery makes a wide range of fantastic breads, including spelt and rye, and cakes. Also some sandwiches and pastries. Everything at this branch is veggie, while at Tapa Coffeehouse (next section) it's 50% veggie. There are sample menus on the website, but lots more available especially for vegans, and daily specials. Almost all ingredients are organic. Gluten-free options. 6 tables and some window seats.

Light breakfast around £1.95-£3 such as muesli with soya milk, beans on toast, toast and spreads, their own bagels.

Meals focus on soups and salads plus some specials. Two soups daily which are always gluten-free and one or both vegan, £3.85 eat in, around £3 takeaway. 4 or 5 sandwiches each day from

a repertoire of 9 recipes, £4.50 eat in or £3.25 take-away, half vegan such as sausage with homemade onion relish, mustard and spinach; hummus and roast red peppers and onions; falafel. Hot and cold specials £5.84 eat in, £4.15 take-away, comes with bread, such as couscous and artichoke salad with pomegranate dressing; pasta salad with broccoli and red pestol; hot Jamaican bean stew; mushroom stroganoff.

Cakes £1.95-3.50 include vegan chocolate and almond torte, summer berry and polenta cake, fruit and nut slice.

Hot drinks £1.85-1.95 for a pot of tea or long black coffee; cappuccino , latte, mocha £2.45. Soya milk 40p extra. No alcohol at this branch.

Their shop section sells bread which is mostly vegan and certified organic. Organic groceries such as home baking supplies, jams, tahini, nut butters, juices, tinned veg and beans. Coffee beans. Cleaning products by BioD and Faith in Nature soaps.

The Bakehouse runs baking classes and Transition Scotland runs Stitch Up events to upcycle clothes, permaculture events and other eco-type activities. There are kids' craft classes downstairs twice a week.

Children's options, high chairs, baby-change and toys. Some outdoor seating. No smoking. Outside catering such as sandwich platters, buffets. MC, Visa.

Glasgow omnivorous cafes

Tapa Coffeehouse

Omnivorous cafe

721 Pollockshaws Rd, Stathbungo, Glasgow (south side) G41 2AA
Tel: 0141-423 9494
Open: Mon–Wed 08.00–18.00,
Thu–Sat 9.00–21.00, Sun 9.00–18.00
www.tapacoffeehouse.com

While the Tapa Bake House (previous section) is completely vegetarian, this second branch is over 50% veggie, has a busy atmostphere, and specialises in good coffee, with more space in the kitchen to offer a bigger range of cooked food. Almost all ingredients are organic. Lots of gluten-free, wheat-free options and they are used to making and adapting lots of dishes for vegans, for example with pine nuts or cashew. Cakes and hot drinks are the same at both branches. Coffee for both branches is roasted here.

Many of the vegetarian dishes on their menu of meals, snacks and breakfasts are with cheese, but vegans can have lots more that isn't on the website: soup £3.75; sandwiches £4.85 such as roast mushroom pate with slow roasted tomatoes, peppers and basil, or falafel with fennel coleslaw crunchy salad, hummus and hot sauce, and other sandwiches can be veganized too; soup and sandwich £7.95, Indian broccoli and green bean starter with tahini dressing £5.65; mains £8.95 such as veg kofta without raita, or spicy puy lentil and pine nut burger £8.95 in a focaccia bun with salad and hand-cut chips; all day vegan Scottish breakfast £8.45 with tofu sausages, tomato, mushrooms, spinach, beans, home-made tattie scone and toast; sausage sandwich £3.60.

Cakes £1.95-3.50 include for vegans (or anyone!) chocolate and almond torte, summer berry and polenta cake, fruit and nut slice.

Hot drinks £1.85-1.95 for a pot of tea or long black coffee; cappuccino, latte, mocha £2.45. Soya milk 40p extra.

All wines and beers are vegetarian organic, most are biodynamic and some vegan both red and white, house wine £15.50 bottle, medium glass £4.95, large £6.95. Samuel Smith's vegan ales £3.10.

Children's portions, high chairs, baby-change and toys. MC, Visa.

Biblocafe

Omnivorous book cafe

262 Woodlands Road, Glasgow G3 6NE
Tel: 0141-339 7645
Open: Sun-Fri 08.30-20.30, Sat-9.30-20.30
www.biblocafe.co.uk
www.facebook.co.uk/biblocafe

Independent coffee house, secondhand bookshop and book-swap. A great place to relax, read or study. They have vegan cakes including Bakewell tart, and vegan gluten-free chocolate cake, shortbread and tiffin. Also a daily vegan soup, sandwiches, juices, coffee, hot choc, teas. Soya milk, no extra charge. Children welcome though not much room for prams. Dogs welcome. Outside tables with umbrellas for smokers. Wifi.

Grassroots Cafe

Organic 90% vegan cafe

1513 Merryhill Road, Merryhill, Glasgow G20 8YE (10-16 minutes walk from centre)
Tel: 0141-
Open: Check website
www.grassrootsorganic.co.uk

Grassroots Organic wholefood store, who used to have a vegetarian cafe years ago, are about to open a new cafe

about 10 minutes walk from the shop, in a centre with offices, artist studios and a garden, next to a sports centre. Community hall next door for catered events such as weddings.

Check their website for full details.

The Left Bank

Omnivorous cafe bar

33-35 Gibson Street, Glasgow G12 8NU
(near Tchai-Ovna)
Tel: 0141 339 5969
Food served: Mon-Fri 9.00-22.00 (drinks until 24.00) Sat & Sun 10-22.00. (drinks until 24.00) Children welcome until 20.00.
www.theleftbank.co.uk

Trendy, bright, place with an imaginative menu. About a quarter vegetarian and many options can be made vegan (these are marked on the menu). Bar snacks around £3-4, full meals £7-14. Veggie breakfast around £7, served 9.30am to midday. The huge snack menu is available midday-10pm and includes soup with bread; hummus with flatbread; salad with beetroot, chick peas and pumpkin seeds; and quinoa super salad.

The evening menu served until 10pm has a vegan thali with cauliflower kofta, daal, rice and black bread for £10.95. Dairy-free ice cream £3.25.

Cocktails £5; bottled beers and soft drinks around £2-4, fair-trade teas and coffees £1.50-£2.35. They have soya milk and vegan smoothies.

Children welcome until 8pm. High chairs. All cards accepted.

The same owners have another licensed restaurant in the West End called **The Two Figs** at 5 and 9 Byers Road G11 5RD. Tel: 0141-334 7277. Menus with veggie dishes marked at www.thetwofigs.co.uk.

Glasgow Indian restaurants

Glasgow has won Curry Capital of Britain four times, most recently in 2010, and is said to have more Indian restaurants than anywhere else. A Glaswegian can practically roll out of bed into one! We've listed a few recommended by local vegetarians.

Assams

Omnivorous Indian restaurant

57 West Regent Street, Glasgow G2 2AE
(near Buchanan Street and central station)
Tel: 0141-331 1980 / 332 3007
Open: Mon–Thu 12.00–23.00,
Fri–Sat 12.00–24.00,. Sun 14.00–23.00
(23.00 last orders)
www.assams.co.uk

Modern Indian restaurant with lots of veggie options, and plenty more they can knock up if you ask, they just can't list everything or the menu would be 20 pages long. Quite swish, with table-cloths and elegant presentation. The staff are very vegan–aware and can easily adapt dishes.

A la carte starters £4 include samosas, aubergine fritters and pakoras. Mains £7.95 (take–away £5.50) include veg karahi, tarka dal, bindi aloo, or tell them your favourite vegetables and they will make something for you.

Tapas menu for groups of friends to share with 9 veggie dishes £2.95–3.95 such as aubergine and potato fritters, dal, samosas, garlic mushroom pakora, okra and potatoes, aloo gobi or whatever you'd like them to make.

Desserts £3.95 but nothing vegan at the moment, though after talking with them we think you could probably encourage them to get in a tub of Swedish Glace. Lunch buffet Mon–Sat 12.00–15.00 £6.95 with 3 or 4 vegetarian dishes plus rice and nan. Tapas lunch £7.50 7 days 12–3pm and pre-theatre £9.50 Sun–Thu 3–6.30pm, for any three dishes with rice or nan.

There's a well-stocked bar, but you can also bring your own wine (but not beer, which you can buy from them), corkage £2.50 per bottle wine, sparkling wine £3.50. House wine from £14.95 bottle, £4.95 large glass.

Children's menu £5.50 for three courses. One under-12 for each adult eats free on Sundays. MC, Visa, Amex.

Banana Leaf

Omnivorous South Indian restaurant

76 Old Dumbarton Road, West End, Glasgow G3 8RE
Tel: 0141-334 4445/6
Open: Mon–Sat 11.30–22.30, Sun 11.30–22.30

105 Albert Drive, South Side, Glasgow G41 2SU.
Tel: 0141-323 8682
Open: Mon–Fri 12.00–22.30, Sat-Sun 11.30–22.30
www.thebananaleaf.co.uk

Very cheap, around half veggie. Starters £2.80–£3.50. Lots of dosas £4.70–£6, Uttapam £4. Main course curries around £6. Slightly cheaper at West End branch, and take–away same price in both, but Albert Drive is slightly more expensive to eat in.

Weekend breakfast till 1pm £3.50 such as Upma semolina with curry leaves and lentils, or Ven Pongal rice and lentils. Unusual rice £4.90 such as tomato or tamarind with lentils. Thali £7. Desserts £2.40 include carrot halva made with nuts and sugar.

Orange juice £1.75, hot drinks £1.50. No alcohol.

Nothing special for children. Take–away is significantly cheaper. Albert Drive branch lunch buffet Mon–Fri £3.99. MC, Visa.

Green Chilli Cafe

Omnivorous Indian tapas restaurant

1293 Argyle St, West End, Glasgow G3 8TL
Tel: 0141–337 6378
Open: Tue–Sun 17.00–22.30, Mon closed
www.greenchillicafe.com

New separate vegan menu with 20 dishes £3 to £4 to mix and match such as pakoras, garlic mushroom poori, aubergine fritters, potatoes and aubergine, veg korma with coconut milk, okra, veg bhani. Rice and breads £1–£2.20. Also main course size portions to take away £7.25. Tue–Wed Madness Nights some dishes only £1, and masala dosa only £1.50.
No vegan desserts. House wine £3.50 medium glass, £4.65 large, £14.95 bottle. High chairs. MC, Visa, Amex.

Mr India's Balti & Dosa House

Omnivorous Punjabi restaurant

11 Hyndland Street, off Dumbarton Road
Glasgow G11 5QE
Tel: 0141–334 0084
Open: Sun–Thu 17.00–23.00,
Fri–Sat 17.00–24.00
No website

Popular, old-fashioned, no-frills Indian noted for large portions. 29 veggie dishes prepared separately from the meat. Typically £10 for a curry with rice. No vegan desserts. House wine £13.95 bottle, £4.25 glass. Children welcome, high chairs. MC, Visa, Amex.

KoolBa

Omnivorous Indian restaurant & bar

109–113 Candleriggs, Merchant City, Glasgow G1 1NP.
Tel: 0141–552 2777
Open: Tue–Wed, Sun 17.00–22.00, Thu–Sat 12.00–24.00, Mon closed
www.koolba.com
Facebook: Koolba Indian Restaurant

A new Indian with a Persian twist. They have unusual options like hummus, olives, dips, grilled aubergine, and nan breads such as Peshwari sweet coconut, or garlic coriander. They don't use food colourings or GM products.
Vegetarian starters £3–4 are gluten-free and include hummus; tomato, cucumber and mint salad; vegetable pakora; grilled aubergine; garlic mushrooms. Mains £8–11 include sweet 'n sour patia with courgettes, cauliflower, bitter gourd; Punjabi ginger vegetable curry; mixed vegetable curry. Pre-theatre until 6.30pm, 2 courses for £10.95. 2-course lunch same price comes with free tea or coffee.
Various cakes and ice creams all contain milk, and pistachio baklava may not be vegan, but aafter talking with us they are looking into vegan ice-cream.
House wine £4.75–£5 large glass, £12.95 bottle. Lots of beers from around Europe and the world. Children's portions, high chairs. MC, Visa, Amex.

Little Italy

Omnivorous Italian restaurant

205 Byres Road, Glasgow G12 8TN
Tel: 0141–339 6287
Open: Mon–Thu 08.00–22.00, Fri–Sat 08.00–
01.00, Sun 10.00–22.00
www.littleitalyglasgow.com
facebook.com/pages
/Little–Italy/140143622747664

Friendly, cheap Italian restaurant near the university that gets lots of veggie customers. If you're vegan, just say when ordering because they make things like salads and pizzas to order. Minestrone soup £3.80, Napoli and arrabbiata pasta £3.95. Basic pizzas £2.95 for a slice, £4.95 10 inch, £6.50 12 inch, £8.50 16 inch one, same price for gluten-free, can be without cheese, wide range of vegetable toppings each 60p/90p, £1.10/£1.60.

Coffee and hot choc from £1.20 to £2.50 for a large cappuccino. They have soya milk. They now sell alochol, wine from £3.50 glass, Italian beers £3.25–3.95.

Children welcome, high chairs and nappy changing facilities. MC, Visa, Amex.

Pizza Express, Glasgow

Omni pizza restaurant & take–away

151 Queen Street, Glasgow G1 3BJ
Tel: 0141–221 3333
Open: Mon–Sun 11.30–22.30

436 Sauchiehall Street, Glasgow G2 3JD
Tel: 0141–332 6965
Open: Mon–Sun 11.30–22.30

15 Xscape Centre, Braehead, Renfrew PA4 8XQ. Tel: 0141–886 4996
Open: Mon–Sun 11.30–22.00
www.pizzaexpress.com for menus and ingredient lists with vegan suitability

This is the description referred to for other branches of this national chain.
Pizza Express is open long hours and is a handy standby. Pizzas have vegan bases and can be made without cheese. In some branches you can bring your own vegan cheese, though they don't stock it. Starters £2.30–2.95 include roasted tomatoes with herbs and olive oil; (marinated) olives; salted Marcona almonds. The new rosemary pizza bread £4.95 is vegan and good for sharing, a large thin pizza base with rosemary, garlic, olive oil, chilli flakes and rock salt. Pizzas £6.95–10.70, such as Veneziana £7.25 with red onions, capers, sultanas and pine kernels. Desserts £4.95 are all based on dairy ice–cream.

Wine from £3.90 medium glass, £4.95 large, £13.40 bottle. Italian beers from £3.55 (330ml bottle). Low alcohol lager £2.70. Spirits £2.60. Soft drinks £2.05–2.80. Tea and coffee £1.70–2.50.

Children welcome and they have their own menu.

Vegetarian but not vegan items marked on menu, so consult the very detailed allergies list or their website if you have a problem with nuts, garlic, tomatoes etc. Vegans beware that some items that are normally vegan in other restau-rants aren't here such as garlic bread and bruschetta. However the chain as a whole are more aware of vegan needs than most restaurants.

Nanakusa

Japanese restaurant

441 Sauchiehall Street, Glasgow G2 3LG
(Charing Cross end)
Tel: 0141–332 6303
Open: Mon–Thu 12.00–14.30, 17.00–23.00;
Fri–Sat 12.00–24.00; Sun 17.00–23.00
www.nanakusa.co.uk

Although it's billed as a grill restaurant, they also have lots of vegetarian rice and noodle dishes and sushi, including miso soup £2; vegetable pancake rolls £2.90; grilled vegetable skewers £2.90; tempura £3.50; edamame £2.90; and several tofu noodle options £7.50–7.90 with fried ramen noodles and for £1 extra you can usually swap for udon buckwheat noodles. Various side dishes and pickles, also bento boxes and sushi with fish–free options including avocado. Vegetarian set lunch £6.95 for miso soup, yasai tempura veg with curry sauce and rice. Various Japanese drinks including unlimited green tea £1.50 and brown rice tea £1.50. Usual teas and coffees around £2. No soya milk. House sake and plum wine £4 for 200ml, premium bottles £18–31.50.
Children welcome. High chairs. MC, Visa, Amex.

Wagamama, Glasgow

Omnivorous Japanese restaurant

97–103 West George Street, Central Glasgow
G2 1PB. Tel: 0141–229 1468
Open: Mon–Sat 12–23.00 Sun 12.30–22.00

Silverburn Centre, Barrhead Road, South Glasgow G53 6AF. Tel: 0141–880 5877
Open: Mon–Sat 12–22.00, Sun 12.30–21.00
www.wagamama.com

Big, busy, noisy restaurants that are great fun with huge portions of the soupy noodle dishes. Vegans should go for rice noodles or thick udon wheat noodles which are egg–free; ask your server for the vegan list. All dishes listed below are either vegan or can be modified. Yasai means vegetables in Japanese.
Miso soup with Japanese pickles £1.55. Steamed edamame green soybeans £4.10. Raw salad £3.20. Main course noodle dishes £7.10–8.70 come in a big bowl and will really fill you up, such as saien soba whole wheat noodles in a vegetable soup topped with fried tofu, beansprouts, courgettes, asparagus, red onion, leeks, mushrooms, mangetout and garlic, garnished with spring onion; yasai yaki soba teppan-fried whole wheat noodles with lots of veg; yasai chilli men stir–fried whole wheat noodles with tofu and veg in a spicy chilli men sauce.
Desserts mostly contain dairy products but they now have fruit ice lollies £1.75. However we've always been totally stuffed anyway after their massive soup–noodle dishes.
Green tea free with meals on request. Other teas £1.50. Coffees £1.55–2.20. Various raw, fresh juices £3.20–4.35. Soft drinks around £2. Peach iced tea £1.70. Japanese beer £3.85–£6.75. Wine from £3.65 glass £12.95 bottle. Sake for one £5.55, to share £8.70. Plum wine £3.60 with ice and water. Kids' portions £3.30–3.90, colouring in sheet and games. MC, Visa.

The Bay Tree

Omnivorous Persian restaurant

403 Great Western Road, Kelvinbridge
Glasgow G4 9HY
Tel: 0141-334 5898
Open: Mon–Sat 9.00–21.30 (last order
21.00), Sun 9.30–20.30
www.baytreecafe.com

A very long–established middle eastern
place that used to be totally vegetarian
and still has loads of veggie dishes.
Long opening hours. Separate vegetarian and vegan menu with main
dishes £8.20 such as hummus falafel
with tortilla bread and mixed salad; or
Arabian aubergine bake with rice or
couscous and mixed salad; Arabian
korma sabzy. Filled baked potato and
mixed salad £4.35. They also have basic
stuff like chips and potato wedges. Unli-
censed, BYO no corkage. Children
welcome, high chair. Free wifi. MC, Visa.

Falafel Petra

Omnivorous Lebanese restaurant

27 Gibson Street, Glasgow G12 8NX
(near Tchai-Ovna)
Tel: 0141-334 1414
Open: Mon–Sun 10.00–22.00
www.falafelpetra.com

Jordanian style and loved by the local
vegan group for its new vegan menu.
Starters £2.50-3.50 include hummus,
falafel, moutabal grilled aubergine
puree with tahini, salads, batata hara
fried potato with spices, dolma, lentil
soup.
Main course £7.95 lots of diferent
veg with Lebanese style rice with
Indian flavour and some rice.
Desserts fruit salad £2.50.
Smoothies and fresh juices £2-2.50.
Soft drinks £1.25. Tea, mint tea, coffee

and Arabic coffee £1.70–1.95. No
alcohol, bring your own, corkage £3 per
bottle of wine, no charge for beer.
Children welcome, high chairs. MC,
Visa.

Cafe La Padella

Omnivorous Middle Eastern cafe

124 Woodlands Road, Glasgow G3 6HB
Tel: 0141-332 6104
Open: Mon-Thu 9.00-21.00,
Fri-Sat 9.00-23.00, Sun 9.00-20.00
www.cafelapadella.co.uk

A bright, turquoise place with a middle
eastern and mediterranean menu that's
about a quarter veggie. All dishes come
with salad. 40 seats, and take–away. It's
great value and we hear portions are
substantial.
All day veggie cooked breakfast £4.50
includes coffee or tea and toast.
Hummus salad hot wrap £3. Meze
£3.50-£5 such as hummus with black
olives and bread, Manca grilled veg
salad, Patlican Begendi aubergine,
guacamole, gado gado beans with
avocado and tomato salad and chilli
dressing; Tarator spicy aubergine with
nuts, chickpeas and sesame seed bread.
Mixed meze for two £10. Pizzas £5.50
take–away, eat in £6.50, can be without
cheese. Baked potato with hummus or
guacamole £3.70. Guacamole is vegan.
Cakes and ice–creams are not vegan.
Coffee, latte, cappuccino, hot choc £2-
2.60, no soya milk but they can get it if
you ask. Tea £1.40. Lots of herbal and
fruit teas £1.30. Juices and soft drinks
£1.40-1.70.
Children welcome. Bring your own wine,
no corkage charge. Some outside tables
in summer, but no dogs. MC, Visa.

Grassroots Organics

Omnivorous supermarket and deli

20 Woodlands Rd, **Charing Cross**, Glasgow
G3 6UR
Tram: St Georges Cross SPT subway station
Tel: 0141-353 3278
Mon–Wed 8.30–18.30, Thu–Fri 8.30–19.00,
Sat 9.00–18.00, Sun 11.00–17.00
www.grassrootsorganic.co.uk

Glasgow's long-established organic supermarket is no longer entirely veggie (there's a meat counter), but still has stacks of great stuff.

The deli has lots of ready made dishes you can take home to heat up, and there are always vegan options. At present it's take-away only but they are looking into getting some seats.

Organic fruit and veg and organic box scheme. Baked goods include bread, focaccia, cakes. They have lots of raw products and even a raw baker producing lots of raw cakes and puddings.

Vegan chocolate heaven with Divine, Conscious raw, Montezuma, Mulu, Plamil, Booja Booja, Dairy Free buttons. Huge chilled section with everything you could want such as vegan cheeses, meat substitutes, 40 kinds of tofu. A whole freezer of ice-cream including vegan Swedish glace, Booja Booja, Wot No Dairy, Coconice (from Dragon's Den).

Organic wine and beer is 90% vegan.

Bodycare includes Vogel, Weleda, Jason, Dr Bronner and refills, John Masters, Natracare, Earth Friendly Baby, Green Baby.

Supplements include Pukka Herbs, Viridian, Higher Nature, Terra Nova, Nature's Answer and A. Vogel/Bioforce. Homeopathy, Bush Flower essences, Findhorn remedies, essential oils.

Cleaning by BioD, Ecover, Ecoleaf and refills for all of these. Gifts such as Pacifica perfumes, incense, burners, cards, candles.

Therapies and clinic dept with massage, shiatsu, hydrothermic massage, exfoliating herb massage, Indian Head, sinus steam massage, beauty treatments, homeopathy, cognitive behavioural therapy, hypnotherapy.

Lots of instore events listed on their website. Tours of the shop last Thursday of the month for 90 minutes at 7pm, ideal if you're new to wholefoods, changing diet, want to know more about the products or just bewildered by the huge range; you can ask questions and there's even a quiz at the end with prizes. Tickets £5, redeemable against purchases.

Vegetarian outside catering and cakes for any occasion. MC, Visa.

Jan de Vries, Shawlands

Health food shop

43 Kilmarnock Road, **Shawlands**, Southside,
Glasgow G41 3YN
Tel: 0141-632 7429
Open: Mon–Sat 9.15–17.30, Sun closed
www.jandevrieshealth.co.uk

The larger of the two Glasgow stores, at
least twice the size of West End branch,
with a bigger range of wholefoods,
supplements and bodycare. Fridge has
drinks and omega oils only, but there
are lots of nearby cafes for lunch. No
freezer. Vegan chocolate by Plamil,
Divine, Moo Free, Nakd, sometimes
Booja Booja.
Bodycare by Faith in Nature, Weleda,
Green People, Barefoot, Pukka,
Natracare, and children's and baby
ranges.
Supplements by Solgar, Bioforce,
Lamberts, Pukka, Quest, Lifeplan, sports
nutrition. Homeopathy, Jan de Vries,
essential oils. Aromatherapist and Jan
de Vries sometimes in store, and allergy
testing. Staff are very knowledgable and
can give advice.
Cleaning by Ecover, Method, Attitude.
Jan de Vries books. Magnetic bracelets.
MC, Visa.

Jan de Vries Health

Health food shop

29 Clarence Drive, **West End**, Glasgow
G12 9QN. Tel: 0141-339 0345
www.jandevrieshealth.co.uk

Small shop with a few grains, nuts,
herbal teas, nut butters, nuts and dried
fruit, snack bars, plant milks, fruit and
vegetable juices, oats, cereals, rice
cakes. No fridge or freezer or take-
aways, but you can get food to go at
Peckhams deli a few doors away.
Bodycare by Weleda, Barefoot Botani-
cals, Planet Health, Avalon, Faith in
Nature, Natracare, Toms, Arran
Aromatics, Dead Sea Magik, Weleda
Baby and Green Baby.
Supplements by Solgar, Quest, Solo,
Nature's Aid, Better You, Optima,
Lamberts, Pharmanord, A. Vogel. Jan de
Vries herbs, vitamins, homeopathy and
some Weleda homeopathy. Natural By
Nature essential oils. Vega food sensi-
tivity testing sometimes available, and
Jan de Vries in shop every other month.
Cleaning by Ecover. All the Jan de Vries
books, relaxation CDs and tapes.
Candles, incense. They can order in
anything else you need. MC, Visa.

Quality Vitamins & Herbs

Health food shop

123 Douglas Street (the one off Sauchiehall Street), Glasgow G2 4HF
Tel: 0141-331 2984
Open: Mon–Sat 9.00–18.00, Sun closed
www.qualityvitamins.co.uk

Organic wholefoods. The shop is all vegetarian apart from a few supplements. They specialise in gluten/wheat-free such as bread and sugar-free. Huge range of herbal teas such as Pukka, Yogi, Dr Stuart.

Fridges with take-away pasties, local veggie haggis, Bute Island and Tofutti vegan cheese, Redwood, vegan yogurts, hummus, lots of tofu products such as Taifun. No freezer.

Vegan choc by Montezuma, Moo Free, Organica, Plamil, Divine, Booja Booja.

Bodycare by Weleda, Green People, Faith in Nature, Jason, Inika vegan organic makeup from Australia, Natracare, Weleda and Green People baby.

Lots of supplements by Viridian, Solgar, Higher Nature, Biocare, Quest, Nature's Own, Nature's Aid, Pukka ayurvedic herbs, Floradix, Lamberts, Nature's Plus etc, and sports nutrition, hemp protein. Weleda homeopathy and Nelson's creams, Absolute Aromas and Country Harvest essential oils. Cleaning products by Ecover. Health books. They can order in anything else you need, e.g. a 25kg bag of rice. MC, Visa, Amex.

Roots & Fruits Wholefoods & Organics

Omnivorous organic shop & deli

453 Great Western Rd, **West End**, Glasgow G12 8HH
wholefoods: 0141-339 3077
flowers: 0141-339 5817
fruit & veg: 0141-334 3530
Train: Kelvinbridge underground
Open: Mon–Fri 07.30–18.30, Sat 8.30–18.30, Sun 09.30–18.00
www.rootsfruitsandflowers.com

This is the original and larger branch with more wholefoods. Massive selection of teas. There is a hot food counter and deli with lunches £2-3.50, ready made and to order such as sandwiches such as hummus with red pepper, chickpea pies, savoury tarts, dolmades, salads, veggie sausage rolls, vegan pesto pasta, coconut spicy beany Thai wraps, stuffed mushrooms. Watch out for meat in some dishes that look veggie at first glance, but there's loads for veggies and vegans. Different vegan cake slices every day £1.60 such as spiced almond and sultana.

Opens very early as they have a super-duper new coffee machine to get your day off to a really good start, and they've added some bar seating inside and four tables outside (dogs welcome there). Coffees, latte, cappuccino £1.30-2.00 drink in or take-away. They have soya milk.

Small range of organic fruit and veg, such as from Pillars of Hercules in Fife, and they have a regular fruit and veg shop next door at 451. They also supply fruit and veg to hotels and restaurants. Chegworth juices all year, apples in autumn.

Fresh bread daily, some organic, some wheat-free, and a long-life gluten-free. Fridge with vegan cheese by Tofutti, Bute Island, Redwood and meat substitutes, hummus, lots of tofu including smoked and marinated, pasties, falafels, soya yogurt.

Freezer with vegan ice-cream by Swedish Glace, Tofutti, Booja Booja.

Vegan chocolate by Plamil, Moo Free, Divine, Organica, Montezuma, Booja Booja.

Bodycare by Faith in Nature, Caurnie soap, Jason, Weleda, Urtekram, Natracare, baby stuff. They don't sell supplements. A few essential oils. No alcohol. Cleaning by Ecover and refills, BioD. Visa, MC.

They have a florist next door at 459 called Roots, Fruits & Flowers. Flower delivery.

Roots & Fruits Whole-foods & Organics, Argyle St

Omnivorous wholefood shop & deli

1137 Argyle St, **Kelvingrove**, Glasgow G3 8ND
Tel: 0141-229 0838
Open: Mon-Fri 08.45-19.30, Sat 08.45-19.00, Sun 10.30-18.00
www.rootsfruitsandflowers.com

This branch opened up when another closed in Byres Road (after Waitrose set up next door). Massive range of veggie food, with a similar range to the other store, plenty for vegans and gluten-free.

There is a hot food counter and deli with lunches around £2.50-4.00, ready made and to order, take-away only, such as sandwiches like hummus salad, and in boxes around £1.20 per 100 grams by weight, such as spicy potato wedges, two veggie soups, salads such as couscous with roast veg or quinoa or mixed bean, veggie sausage rolls, chickpea pies, savoury tarts (sometimes vegan), dolmades, vegan pesto pasta. Watch out for meat in some dishes that look veggie at first glance, but there's loads for veggies and vegans. Different vegan cake slices every day £1.60 such

as pineapple and poppy seed. Coffees, latte, cappuccino £1.80-2.00. They have soya milk.

Fruit & veg (not organic at this branch). Chegworth juices. Their speciality is fresh bread daily from six different bakeries, some organic, including spelt and rye, and a long-life gluten-free.

Fridge with Tofutti creamy vegan cheese, Redwood tempeh rashers and Vegideli Lincolnshire sausages, veggie burgers, MacSween vegan haggis, hummus, lots of tofu including smoked and marinated and Engine Shed, Jordan Valley and Ishtar vegan pasties (both from Edinburgh), falafels, soya yogurt. No freezer.

Vegan chocolate by Divine, Montezuma, Booja Booja.

No supplements or alcohol. Bodycare at the other shop. Cleaning by Ecover, refills at the other store. Visa, MC.

Whole Foods Market

Omnivorous wholefoods supermarket, greengrocer, bakery and cafe

124–134 Fenwick Road, Giffnock, Glasgow
G46 6XN
Tel: 0141–621 2700
Open: Mon–Sat 08.00–21.00,
Sun shorter hours
www.wholefoodsmarket.com

Big new store, 20,000 square feet and 140 staff, opened November 2011. There is a range of healthy and fresh foods, including a greengrocers, with a wet rack of green produce, huge range of seasonal fresh green vegetables. Lots of organic fruit and veg, much of it sourced from local producers. Bulk section where you measure out your own pulses, grains, seeds etc. No artificial preservatives, colours, flavours, sweeteners or hydrogenated fats.
In house from scratch bakery, certified kosher, with a range of speciality breads, focaccia, ciabatta and lots of cakes, including vegan and gluten–free. 34–seat cafe with a deli and take–away, coffee bar, juice bar, sushi bar, salad bar, *Health Starts Here* prepared salad bar, soup station, Stoats Oats porridge bar where you can make up your own porridge toppings, DIY burritos.
Whole Body section has organic skin, body and hair care including their own Whole Body exclusive brands that are new to the UK: Danish Unique Hair Care and Rudolph Care (from acai), MyChelle from USA, i+m Naturkosmetik vegan range from Germany, Greenland raw range from the Netherlands, 66/30degrees from France. Lots of supplements and an in–house herbalist to advise.
Baby foods and products. Wine, whisky and beer, some in refillable flagons and carafes. Cleaning products.

Customer parking for 60 cars on roof and more opposite the store. Special events such as product tastings, makeup masterclasses. MC, Visa, Amex.

Holland & Barrett, Strathclyde

Health food shop

9 Queen Street, Central Glasgow G1 3ED
Tel: 0141–221 3425
Open: Mon–Sat 9.00–18.00, Thu 19.00, Sun
12.00–18.00

94 Sauchiehall Street, Central Glasgow G2
3DE
Tel: 0141–331 1188
Open: Mon–Sat 8.30–18.00, Thu 19.00,
Sun 11.00–17.30

Unit C10, **Glasgow Fort Shopping Centre**,
Lanarkshire G33 5AL. Tel: 0141–773 3605
Open: Mon–Fri 10.00–21.00, Sat 9.00–18.30,
Sun 10.00–18.00

Unit 40, **Parkhead Forge, Glasgow** G31 4EB
Tel: 0141–551 8420
Open: Mon–Sat 9.00–17.30, Sun 11–17.00

Silverburn, Unit W5, Barrhead Road, Glasgow,
Lanarkshire G53 6QR. Tel: 0141–881 3632
Open: Mon–Fri 10.00–21.00, Sat 9.00–18.00,
Sun 10.00–18.00

14 Douglas St, **Milngavie**, Glasgow G62 6PB
Tel: 01419–551 542
Open: Mon–Sat 9.00–17.30, Sun 11–16.00

Unit 55 **Braehead** Shopping Centre, Kings Inch
Road, **Renfrew**, Renfrewshire G51 4BS
Tel: 0141–886 5393
Open: Mon–Fri 10.00–21.00, Sat 9.00–18.30,
Sun 10.00–18.00

Unit 23, Hamilton Way, **Greenock**,
Renfrewshire PA15 1JJ
Tel: 01475–552 553
Open: Mon–Sat 9.00–17.30, Sun 11–16.00

37a The Avenue at Mearns, 250 Ayr Road,
Newton Mearns, East Renfrewshire G77 6EY
Tel: 0141–639 5432
Open: Mon–Sat 9.00–18.00, Sun 11–17.00

45 Sylvania Way, **Clyde Shopping Centre**,
Clydebank, Dunbartonshire G81 2RR
Tel: 0141–952 8644
Open: Mon–Sat 9.00–17.30, Sun 12–16.00

11 High Street, **Lanark**, South Lanarkshire
ML11 7LN. Tel: 01555–661 449
Open: Mon–Sat 9.00–17.30, Sun closed

Unit 30 Antonine Centre, Tryst Rd,
Cumbernauld, Lanarkshire G67 1JW
Tel: 01236–724 313
Open: Mon–Sat 9.00–18.00, Sun 12–17.00

9 Duke Street, **Hamilton**, South Lanarkshire
ML3 7DT. Tel: 01698–281 356
Open: Mon–Sat 9.00–17.30, Sun 12–16.00

34 Brandon Parade South, **Motherwell**, North
Lanarkshire ML1 1RB
Tel: 01698–230 929
Open: Mon–Sat 9.00–17.30, Sun 12–16.00

Unit 23, The Olympia, **East Kilbride**, South
Lanarkshire G74 1PG. Tel: 01355–232 627
Open: Mon–Sat 9.00–17.30, Thu 19.00, Sun
11.00–17.00

66 Graham Street, **Airdrie**, North Lanarkshire
ML6 6DB. Tel: 01236–751 551
Open: Mon–Sat 9.00–17.30, Sun closed

Unit 2, The Cross, **Paisley**, Renfrewshire PA1
2AS. Tel: 0141–848 5989
Open: Mon–Sat 9.00–17.30, Sun 12–16.00

61 High St, **Dumbarton** G82 1LS
Tel: 01389–730 754
Open: Mon–Sat 9.00–17.30, Sun closed
www.hollandandbarrett.com

National chain of health food shops that
sell bagged dried foods, supplements
and vitamins. Lots of muesli, nuts, dried
fruit, flapjacks and sweets. City centre
and shopping centre branches usually
have a fridge and are good to grab
lunch on the run such as vegetarian
sausage rolls, pies, pasties and
Jamaican patties.

Imrie Fruit

Greengrocer and grocer

8 The Avenue at Mearns, **Newton Mearns**, Glasgow G77 6EY
Tel: 0141–639 6619
Open: Mon–Sat 8.00–17.30,
Sun 9.00–17.00
Facebook: Imrie Fruit

61 Main Street, **Thornliebank**, Glasgow G46 7RX
Tel: 0141–620 0869
Open: Mon–Sat 9.00–17.30, Sun closed

East Kilbridge Shopping Centre, The Plaza, **East Kilbride** G74 1LW
Tel: 01355–231 000
Open: Mon–Fri 8.30–17.30 Sun closed

Proper greengrocers with a big selection of fruit from oranges to loganberries and papaya, and flowers.
The huge main shop at Newton Mearns also sells a lot of wholefoods from Green City, fruit baskets and hampers. The other smaller stores sell chutneys, and East Kildbride shopping centre has some cakes (not vegan).

Lush

Cruelty–free cosmetics shop

111 Buchanan Street, Glasgow G1 3HF
Tel: 0141–243 2522
Open: Mon–Wed 9.30–18.00, Thu 9.30–19.00, Fri–Sat 9.30–18.30, Sun 11.00–18.00

136 Sauchiehall Street, Glasgow G2 3ER
Tel: 0141–333 9912
Open: Mon–Sat 10.00–17.00, Sun 11.00–16.00

Unit 140b Braehead Shopping Centre, Kings Inch Rd, Braehead G51 4BS
Tel: 0141–885 2166
Open: Mon–Fri 10.00–21.00, Sat 9.00–18.30, Sun 10.00–18.00 (longer hours at Christmas)
www.lush.co.uk

Lively, colourful and strongly–scented vegetarian cosmetics store. Vegan products are clearly labelled.

Green City Wholefoods

Vegetarian food wholesaler

23 Fleming St, Dennistoun (East End),
Glasgow G31 1PQ
Tel: 0141–554 7633
Open: Mon–Fri 9.00–17.00, Fri –15.00
www.greencity.co.uk

A huge, well-stocked vegetarian
wholefood co-op, no longer cash and
carry. Minimum order £10 if you collect.
Minimum order for delivery £100 to
central Edinburgh or Glasgow. If you're
an individual in these areas, best to
enquire about bulk buying at one of the
wholefoods stores they supply.

Lazy Day Foods Ltd

Vegan cake and biscuit bakery

1 Moncrieffe Road, Chapelhall Industrial
Estate, Chapelhall, North Lanarkshire, ML6
8QH (off the M8 on the way to Edinburgh)
Tel: 01236–765 300
Open: Not currently open to callers
www.lazydayfoods.comonline shop

Not a shop you can visit, but wholesale
and online retail vegan and wheat-free
biscuits and cakes, sold by stores in this
book including Roots & Fruits and the
new Whole Foods Market, plus Real
Foods in Edinburgh and others supplied
by Green City. Also in Waitrose, Sains-
burys, Dobbies garden centre shops
and restaurants across Scotland
(Aberdeen, Ayr, Dundee, Dunfermline,
Lasswade on Edinburgh outskirts,
Stirling) and some National Trust for
Scotland cafes.
The chocolate fudge cake, available only
online, comes highly recommended
and has won awards.

Glasgow local groups

Vegan Edinburgh + Glasgow

Online resource

Facebook: Vegan Edinburgh + Glasgow
www.facebook.com/groups/
106588816094435

This is a group for vegans, and people thinking about becoming vegan, in the central belt of Scotland.

Glasgow University Vegan Society

Local student group

Vegan Society of the University of Glasgow,
University of Glasgow, G12 8QQ
www.gla.ac.uk/clubs/vegan
www.glasgow.ac.uk/clubs/vegan
Facebook: Glasgow Uni Food Co-op
email: vegan-info@glasgow.ac.uk

An active group for university staff and students who are vegan, aspiring vegans or supporters of the provision of vegan food. Regular sessions in cafes. The website has a Vegan Guide to Glasgow. Also a food bulk buying co-op open to non-students.

The group has persuaded the university to have good vegan options all the time in the canteen in the Gilbert Scott main building (the big fairy-tale castle building), which is open to the public, but closed weekends The address is:
One A The Square (OATS) Brasserie
1A The Square
University of Glasgow
Glasgow G12 8QQ
The Brasserie is open 8.30-14.30, hot meals from 11.30. Full breakfast range, baked potatoes, baguettes, vegan soup and main course always on offer, coffees and speciality teas.
The Cafe is open 10.00-16.30 with newspapers, speciality tea and coffee, flavoured latte, soya milk options, Fairtrade hot chocolate.

Glasgow Raw Food

Online group who host events

www.meetup.com/Glasgow-Raw-Food

Anyone interested in the raw food diet and lifestyle is welcome at their potluck meals.

Aberdeen is the hub of the North Sea oil industry and ferry port for the northern isles. It lacks the cosmopolitan bustle of Edinburgh and Glasgow and has more of an overgrown village feel. Tourists use the city as a base from which to explore the Cairngorms and the rugged coastline. Aberdeen has a distinctive look due to all the granite buildings, which sparkle in the sun. There's an ancient university, free museums and art galleries, a cathedral, Stratosphere science and discovery centre, and the Codonas Amusement Park where the big wheel offers views of the city.

Aberdeen is the gateway to the Malt Whisky Trail and the Castle Trail. A short drive away at Cruden Bay are the ruins of Slains Castle, which inspired Bram Stoker's *Dracula*. The area has miles of rugged beaches with sand dunes and pine forests, footpaths for all abilities in the Grampian hills, and many neolithic stone circles. The edge of the Cairngorms National Park is about an hour away.

Stonehaven is a nearby coastal town, which hosts an awe-inspiring fireball parade every Hogmanay. The Aberdeenshire coast has many great sites for spotting dolphins, seals and seabirds, which, combined with forests further inland full of red squirrels and stags, makes the area an ideal destination for nature-lovers.

Aberdeen is well-connected by road and rail and has an airport. Ferries run to Orkney and Shetland.

Tourism info:
www.aberdeen-grampian.com
www.maltwhiskytrail.com

Aberdeenshire

Aberdeenshire SCOTLAND

Atholl Hotel

Omnivorous hotel

54 King's Gate, Aberdeen AB15 4YN
01224–323 505
Train: Aberdeen 30 mins walk, 10 mins taxi
or bus
www.atholl–aberdeen.co.uk

Privately owned hotel with a large, pleasant dining room, open to non-residents and they do bar lunches. It's 5 minutes by car from the centre or 20 minutes on foot, in a pleasant leafy suburb in the Rosemount district.
En suite single £100 per night Mon–Thu or £60 weekend, double as single £115/£65, double or twin ensuite £130–145/£75–85, family room based on one child £160/£100. Rooms have satellite tv, radio, phone, trouser press, hairdryer, tea and coffee making. Cable internet access in rooms, computer in guest corridor, wifi in lounge.
No lift in this listed building. Large car park. No dogs except guide dogs. High chairs, cots.
The restaurant is open every day for lunch and dinner till 9pm. Menus include vegetarian dishes, around £5.45 –5.75 starter, £10 main and they can cater for vegans. Pot of tea or coffee £2.50. Function rooms.

The Jays Guest House

Omnivorous guest house

422 King Street, Aberdeen AB24 3BR
(corner of Pittodrie Street)
Tel: 01224–638 295
www.jaysguesthouse.co.uk

4–star central bed and breakfast that is used to doing a full cooked breakfast for veggies and vegans – they can get anything you need if you let them know in advance. Open Sun night to Fri morning, though they can be flexible for people staying more than a week.
10 rooms, 8 ensuite and 2 with private facilities. Per person: single £60 or £55 for 2+ nights, double/twin from £50 (£45 for 2+ nights, £65/60 as single). Children 12 or over welcome. No pets. Rooms have clock radio alarms, tea/coffee making, freeview satellite tv, free wifi. Private car park. Certificate of excellence from Trip Advisor, Visit Scotland 4 stars, AA 4 stars.

Roselea House

Omnivorous guest house

12 Springbank Terrace, Aberdeen AB11 6LS
Tel: 01224–583 060
Train and bus station: Aberdeen 10 mins walk
www.roseleahouse.co.uk

Central family run guest house near Union Square bus and railway, and the Northlink ferry terminal for Orkney and Shetland. Single £35, ensuite £44. Per person twin/double £24, double ensuite £28. 0–5 years £14, 6–16 £20, cots, high chairs. Two ground floor rooms good for mobility.
Full cooked vegetarian breakfast, vegan with notice: just let them know what you like; can do gluten-free. Free wifi. Rooms have tv, basin, tea/coffee making. Luggage and bike storage. Payphone. Laptop available for email checking. No pets.

Aberdeen Youth Hostel

Omnivorous hostel

8 Queen's Road, Aberdeen AB15 4ZT
Tel: 01224–646 988
Train: Aberdeen 1.8 miles
Open: all year. Reception 07.00–23.00.
Access to room from 14.00.
www.syha.org.uk

Historic building. 107 beds. Dorm £20.50 (£2 less for Hostelling International members), single £30, double/twin £48, 4–berth £80, 5–berth £98.50.

Continental breakfast £4.20 must be booked and can be vegetarian but not vegan, or just make your own in the self-catering kitchen with fridges. Co-op nearby open till 10pm.

Bicycle storage. Internet £1 per 20 minutes. Wifi. Laundry £2. No pets. No stag or hen parties.

Cranford Guest House

Omnivorous guest house

15 Glenshee Road, Braemar AB35 5YQ
Tel: 013397–41675
Bus from Aberdeen
www.cranfordbraemar.co.uk
Facebook: Cranford Guest House Braemar

In a picturesque village in the Cairngorms National Park, 8 miles from Balmoral castle and close to the start of the Whisky Trail. Ideal for couples, families and groups of friends.

Five rooms, 4 ensuite, one with private bathroom, 3 twin/double, 1 double with child bed, 1 family with double and 2 bunk beds. £27–36 per person, add 50% for single occupancy, children 2–14 half price, under–2 free. Travel cot.

Cooked vegetarian, vegan or gluten-free breakfast. Packed lunches £6.50. Evenings they can provide homemade soup, sandwiches and cakes. Guest lounge with mountaineering and local interest books to browse or borrow.

Detached self-catering cottage with double bedroom £250–475 per week, woodburning stove in the lounge, kitchen/diner and enclosed garden, pets welcome. Good for a couple or with a very young child.

Free wifi. Secure storage for bikes and skis. Drying room and laundry. Car parking. Dogs welcome.

SCOTLAND Aberdeenshire

73

Tropical Gateway Cafe

Vegan cafe & take-away

8-10 Market St, Unit 58 (in the market), Aberdeen AB11 5NX
Tel: 01224-582 131
Open: Mon-Fri 9.00-16.30, Sat-Sun closed
tropicalgatewayvegancafe.wordpress.com
Facebook: Tropical Gateway - Vegan Cafe

Vegan café and take-away opened April 2011 with healthy Caribbean and local food, run by a 7th Day Adventist, so no caffeine or alcohol. Very friendly atmosphere and bargain food.

Light meals (£1.50-£3) such as burgers and hot dogs; sandwiches; soup; and full vegan breakfast. Substantial Jamaican curry £4 - our reviewer found it very tasty and filling.

Fruit and carrot cake £1.50-£2.50. They are looking into flapjacks.

Hot drinks 80p-£1 include Barleycup, ginger tea, herbal teas. Cold drinks 65p-£1.75 include juices, mango and carrot, sorrel and ginger, fruit punch, Bob Marley berry drink, ginger beer, coconut water, Mighty Malt.

Kids welcome. No dogs. Cash only for now. Wifi. Planning health talks and cookery demonstrations.

Many of the veggie-friendly places in Aberdeen are clustered around Belmont Street, an attractive side-street off the main shopping area of Union Street. Belmont Street has a little cinema, pubs, and independent cafes.

The Beautiful Mountain

Omnivorous sandwich cafe

11-13 Belmont Street, Aberdeen AB10 1JR
Tel: 01224-645 353
Open: Mon–Fri 08.00-16.30, Sat 08.00-17.00, also Thu–Sat 17.30-23.00, Sun closed. Closed public holidays.
www.thebeautifulmountain.com

Sandwiches £4-6 (cheaper for take-away) can be made on a range of breads, add 50p for ciabatta or gluten-free bread, with several vegan options such as avocado or hummus with grilled red peppers; peanut butter; spicy bean pate; garlic roasted Mediterranean veg; and hot chickpea fritter. Sandwiches to eat in come with side salad and couscous. Soups £3-4.

Coffee, tea, latte, cappuccino, mocha, hot choc £1.20-2.30, soya milk available. Soft drinks, smoothies, freshly squeezed orange juice 65p-£2.10.

They recently introduced an evening tapas menu with vegetarian and gluten-free dishes marked (£3.35-6.10) such as mixed olives; patatas bravas; green salad; couscous; roast tomato salad; pea and broad bean hummus; mushroom and tarragon croquettes with tomato salsa; or a mixed vege-tarian platter £9.20.

In the evenings, they serve Belgian, German and Czech beers £3-4; organic cider £4; brandy and whisky £3; and wine by the bottle or glass.

Staff are very helpful and vegan-aware.

Books and Beans

Secondhand bookshop with cafe

22 Belmont Street, Aberdeen AB10 1JH
Tel: 01224-646 438
Open: Mon–Sat 7.45-16.30, Sun 9.00-3.30
www.booksandbeans.co.uk

Aberdeen's first independent Fairtrade coffee shop is inside a large bookshop on several floors. Soups, around £3, are almost always vegetarian. Light meals £3-4 such as couscous or pasta salad; sandwiches and panini. The vegan sandwich option is hummus, roast pepper and sundried tomato. All sand-wiches come with coleslaw unless you state otherwise and they sometimes put unexpected cheese on as well. A typical soup and sandwich meal deal is £5.45. Teas £1.85 small pot, £2.95 large. Coffee, latte, cappuccino, mocha, Divine Fairtrade hot choc £1.55-2.35. They have soya milk. Frozen fruity smoothie £2.75. Freshly squeezed orange juice £1.95. Ribena 50p.

Children's menu, high chairs, crayons, lots of kids' books. PCs for internet access. Free poetry evening last Thursday of the month 6.30-8pm.

Three bars in Belmont Street do food (omnivorous) and are open in the evening, with vegetarian dishes but not much for vegans:

Wild Boar, 19 Belmont Street, Tel 01224 625357. Does a Mediterranean vegetable wrap.

Revolution, 25 Belmont Street, Tel 01224 645475 Does a tomato and hummus ciabatta; and a sweet potato and bean falafel wrap that can be made without yoghurt.

Slains Castle, 14-18 Belmont St, Tel 01224 631 877. An eerie theme pub. Serves food 11am 'til midnight. Does baked potato with bean chilli. The veggie burger comes with mayo on it unless you request otherwise.

Blue Moon

Omnivorous Indian restaurant

11 Holburn St, Aberdeen AB10 6BS
Tel: 01224-589 977
Open: Mon–Thu 12.00–14.00, 17,00–
01.00; Fri–Sun 12.00–01.00
www.bluemoon-aberdeen.com

Modern Indian restaurant with lots of vegetarian options. The menu is huge and the staff are vegan-aware. Some unusual dishes, like marrow bhaji.
Starters £4.35 such as garlic mushrooms; baked red pepper stuffed with spicy veg; corn on the cob; or have a platter £6.85 per person with pakora, bhaji, chana puri, samosa and mushroom pakora. All kinds of veg curry £8.75 such as dopiaza, dansak, masala and lots more. Side dishes £4.35. Rice £2.50, breads £3.25.
Business lunch Mon–Fri £6.95 for starter and main. Weekend special menu 12.00–16.00, £7.95 two courses and coffee, £9.95 for three.
Wine from £14.95 bottle. Child portions, high chairs. Take-away 20% cheaper.

Cafe 52

Omnivorous restaurant

52 The Green, Aberdeen AB11 6PE
Tel: 01224-590 094
Open: Mon–Sat 12–24.00, Sun 12–18.00
www.cafe52.net
Facebook: Cafe52

A funky place just off Union St. Some vegetarian dishes on menu and the friendly chefs can make them vegan if you ask. Light meals cost around £5, such as roast butternut squash and wild garlic hummus platter with parsnip chips (can be made without honey on request). Soup £2.50, with flavours like parsnip and apple. Prices go up in December, with larger meals on Christmas menu. Licensed. Free wifi.

The Coffee House

Omnivorous cafe

1 Gaelic Lane, Aberdeen AB10 1JF
(off Belmont Street)
Tel: 07905 160695
Open: Mon–Fri 8.00–20.00,
Sat–Sun 9.00–20.00
www.thecoffeehouseoffers.co.uk

A new cafe with comfy sofas and art on the walls that specialises in local, organic food. Gluten-free options.
Several choices of soup for around £3, typically courgette; butternut squash; and lentil. Roast veg, organic hummus and salad sandwich £4.60.
10% discount for students.

The Foyer

Omnivorous restaurant

82a Crown Street, Aberdeen AB11 6ET
Tel: 01224-582 277
Open: Tue–Sat 11.00–23.30 (last food order 21.30), closed Sun–Mon
www.foyerrestaurant.com

Restaurant with contemporary art in a former church which is run as a fundraiser for a homeless charity. Serves gourmet food, with separate menus for daytime and evening (after 5pm). They also have gluten-free and dairy-free menus for each.
During the daytime, starters are £4–6 and mains around £9 and there's quite a lot of choice for us, with soup; or crostini with wild mushrooms, spinach and rocket salad for starter and mains like beetroot risotto with sage dressing; or squash, tomato and char-grilled pepper salad with lemon-infused oil. Side dishes like chips £3. They have sorbets, plus a mixed fruit platter with orange and cinnamon syrup.
After 5pm the menu becomes more restricted with only one vegetarian option per course and mains go up to £15 minimum.

Little Italy

Omnivorous Italian restaurant

79–81 Holburn Street, Aberdeen AB10 6BR
Tel: 01224–572 240
Open: Mon–Wed 12.00–15.00 and 17.00–22.00, Thu–Sat 12.00–22.30
www.littleitalyaberdeen.co.uk

Authentically Italian place with lots of potential vegan options such as minestrone soup, bruschetta with tomatoes, marinated olives, penne arrabiata, penne Napoli and pizzas with flexible toppings. Just say when ordering if you want your food dairy–free. No vegan desserts. Starters cost around £3–5, main courses around £8–10.

Licensed, with a range of wines. Children welcome, high chairs.

Pizza Express, Aberdeen

Omnivorous restaurant

402 Union Street, Aberdeen AB10 1TQ
Tel: 01224–649 511
Open: Mon–Thu 11.30–22.30,
Fri–Sat 11.30–23.00, Sun 12.00–22.30

Caberstone House, 47 Belmont Street, Aberdeen AB10 1JS
Tel: 01224–620128
Open: Mon–Thu 11.30–22.30,
Fri–Sat 11.30–23.00, Sun 12.00–22.30
www.pizzaexpress.com

For menu see Glasgow.

Rendezvous @ Nargile

Omnivorous Turkish fusion restaurant

106–108 Forest Ave, Aberdeen AB15 4UP
Tel: 01224–323 700
Open 7 days, 12.00 till late. (Time of last orders depends purely on how busy they are, so enquire on booking)
www.rendezvousatnargile.co.uk

Upmarket long–established fusion restaurant with vegan main meals and meze options. They say they can accommodate pretty much any dietary requirement except serious nut allergies, so just ask when booking.

The lunchtime (12.00–16.30) meze menu has all the expected Middle Eastern dishes for £4–7 like baba ghanoush; falafel with tahini dip; hummus; fattoush; tomato soup; also bruschetta. The main courses have much less vegetarian choice and are mostly based on cheese.

The a la carte menu has a vegetarian page with dishes such as couscous and chickpea casserole; roast aubergine kebab; and vegetable casserole in spiced tomato sauce. All around £13–15. Side dishes (around £4) include garlic and rosemary roasted potatoes; marinated olives; and chips.

Wine £3.85–6.55 glass, from £15 a bottle. Large range of whisky and other spirits, £3–6 a glass. Lager £3.25 a bottle. Fizzy drinks and fruit juices around £2.

Rustico

Omnivorous Mediterranean restaurant

62–63 Union Row, Aberdeen, AB10 1SA
Tel: 01224–658 444
Open: Mon–Sat 12.30–14.30 and 17.30–22.30, Sun 17.30–21.00
www.rustico–restaurant.co.uk

Large Mediterranean restaurant divided into smaller rooms to give an intimate feel. The menu is mostly Italian, with quite a wide choice for vegetarians.

Starters (around £3) include garlic bread; bruschetta; and insalata pomedoro (tomato and basil salad). Mains (around £8.50 evenings, £5 daytime) include penne arrabiata; ravioli primavera (roast vegetable ravioli) and several pizzas, which can be prepared without cheese. They have lemon sorbet for dessert.

Licensed, with a bar. Children welcome. high chairs.

Wagamama, Aberdeen

Omnivorous Japanese restaurant

Union Square shopping centre, Guild Square,
Aberdeen AB11 5RG
Tel: 01224–593 056
Open: Mon–Sat 11.30–23.00,
Sun 12.00–22.00
www.wagamama.com

For menus see Glasgow section.

Aberdeen shops

Grampian Health Foods

Health food shop

34 Market Street, Aberdeen AB11 5PL
Tel: 01224–590 886
Open: Mon–Fri 9.00–18.00, Sat 9.00–17.30,
Sun closed
www.grampianhealthstore.co.uk

Gluten-free bread, sometimes fresh
bread. Fridge and freezer with pasties,
sandwiches, vegan cheese, meat
substitutes, vegan ice-cream by Booja
Booja and Swedish Glace. Vegan
chocolate by Plamil, Booja Booja, Divine.
Bodycare by Faith in Nature, Jason,
Weleda, Green People, Natracare,
Weleda Baby.
Supplements by Solgar, Bioforce,
Nature's Plus, Viridian, Quest, Gemini,
Higher Nature. Homeopathy and
remedies, essential oils.
Clinic with Reverse therapy, food sensi-
tivity testing, and bimonthly naturopath
Jan de Vries.
Cleaning by Ecover and refills, Method.
Books and magazines. MC, Visa

Nature's Larder

Wholefood shop

60 Holburn Street, Aberdeen AB10 6BX
Tel: 01224–588 120
Open: Mon–Fri 9.00–18.00, Sat 9.30–18.00,
Sun closed
http://sitebuilder.yell.com/sb/show.do?id=S
B0001730117000040

An astonishing 5,000 items in stock.
Fridge and freezer with vegan cheese
and meat substitutes, tofu, hummus,
vegan ice-cream by Booja Booja. Vegan
chocolate Plamil, Montezuma.
Bodycare by Faith in Nature, Weleda,
Avalon, Jason, Allergenics, Biona,
Natracare.
Supplements by Bioforce, Jan de Vries,
Solgar, Quest, Nature's Aid, FSC, Best.
Essential oils.
Cleaning by Ecover, Attitude, Faith in
Nature and refills, Earth Friendly.
MC, Visa. They can post out orders.

The Nutri Centre

Health food shop

Tesco Extra (a large one), Laurel Drive,
Danestone, Aberdeen AB22 8HB (north side
of the city)
Tel: 01224– 821 536
Open: Mon–Wed 10.00–19.00, Thu–Fri 9.00–
20.00, Sat 9.00–19.00, Sun 10.00–18.00
www.nutricentre.com

Fridge and freezer with vegan cheeses,
burgers, meat replacers, dairy-free ice-
cream and cheesecake. Dairy-free
chocolate by Plamil, Moofree.
Bodycare by Faith in Nature, Jason,
Tisserand etc, some Natracare.
Supplements by Lamberts, Higher
Nature, Nature's Plus, sports nutrition.
Weleda homeopathy, Bach flower
remedies, Tisserand essential oils.
Nutritionist in store. MC, Visa.

Holland & Barrett, Aberdeen

Health food shops

49 Netherkirkgate, **Aberdeen** AB10 1AU
Tel: 01224–648 810
Open: Mon–Sat 9.00–17.30, Sun 11.30–16.30

Aberdeen Trinity, Unit 2 Trinity Centre, 155 Union Street, Aberdeen AB11 6BD
Tel: 01224 581 737
Open: Mon–Sat 9.00–17.30, Sun 11.00–17.00

The Green Grocer

Wholefood shop

76 West High Street, **Inverurie** AB51 3QR
Tel: 01467–620 245
Open: Mon–Sat 9.00–17.30, Sun closed

Traditional grocer and wholefood shop with minimum packaging. Lots of wholefoods, special diets and organic products, soya milk. Fridge with Bute Island, Redwood and Tofutti vegan cheeses, hummus, soya yogurts. Vegetarian but not vegan sausages though you can order these in. Local and organic fruit and vegetable boxes delivered.
Vegan chocolate by Organica, Montezuma, Plamil, Booja Booja, Moo Free.
Bodycare by Faith in Nature, Suma, Weleda, Green People, Earth Friendly Baby, Natracare.
A few supplements. Essential oils. Cleaning by Ecover, Ecoleaf and all the refills for both, BioD.
Gifts such as bamboo socks, candles, locally made charity cards. Homebrew supplies.
Cash only, cashpoint nearby. They can order in weekly anything you need from Green City (see Glasgow) or Suma except frozen.

Grampian Animal Rights

Local group

www.grampianara.org

The website includes a vegan guide to Aberdeen.

Aberdeen Visitor Information Centre

Free tourist information

23 Union Street, Aberdeen
Tel: 01224–288 828
www.aberdeenshire.gov.uk/visit/tourist_info
www.aberdeencity.gov.uk – events calendar

Visit Scotland Aberdeen & Grampian

Free tourist information

Exchange House, 26/28 Exchange Street, Aberdeen AB11 6PH
Tel: 01224–288 828
www.aberdeen–grampian.com
aberdeen.information@visitscotland.com

SCOTLAND Aberdeenshire

Angus

Dundee accommodation

B&B @ Alberta

Omnivorous guest house

51 Forfar Road, Dundee DD4 7BE
Tel: 01382–461 484, 07702 838350
Train: Dundee then bus 32 or 33
www.facebook.com/alberta51
alberta.guesthouse@gmail.com

They say "Stay in a real house with real Scottish people", where vegetarian breakfast is cooked by a vegetarian and they can do vegan too. Single £30, small single £25, twin/double ensuite £27.50–30 per person or £45 as single. Children welcome, travel cot, sometimes high chair. No dogs. Original paintings, illustrations and crafts for sale.

Strathdon Guest House

Omnivorous guest house

277 Perth Road, Dundee DD2 1JS
Tel: 01382–665 648
Open: all year except Xmas, New Year
Train: Dundee 1 mile
strathdon.dundee@tinyworld.co.uk

Family–run guest house in a Victorian terrace with views over the River Tay towards Fife. 8 ensuite rooms, single £31, twin/double £26 per person, family £25 per person. Cot and high chair. Vegetarian cooked breakfast, vegan with notice. Free wifi. No dogs. On street parking. STB 3 stars.

Dundee restaurants

Dundee has no vegetarian restaurants, but the following have veggie and vegan options.

The Parlour Cafe

Omnivorous cafe

58 West Port, Dundee DD1 5ER
Tel: 01382–203 588
Open: Mon–Fri 8.00–19.00, Sat 8.00–17.00,
Sun 10.00–15.00
Facebook: The Parlour Cafe Cookbook

The best place in Dundee for veggies. In the cultural quarter by the university and very popular with non students too. Food is at least 80% vegetarian. The manager is vegetarian and has even published her own cookbook which you can buy here. The menu is flexible, just ask for what you want.

Choice of two soups, £3.50 with bread. The Ottolenghi style vegetarian salad bar is 50% vegan with 8 items plus falafel and vine leaves, £3–4 take–away or have an eat–in meze platter for around £6. Hot dishes include Spanish tortillas, tarts, and blackeye beanburger £7.25 with salad. Weekend brunch menu features full cooked breakfast £6.95 which can even include falafel or sweet potato hash browns.

Sandwiches with salad £4.95–5.95 such as falafel. Cup of soup and toastie £5.50.

Lots of cakes and muffins £1.75–£3, one or two vegan and gluten–free such as satsuma and almond.

Pot of tea £1.45. Coffee, cappuccino, latte £1.35–2.30. They have soya milk. Organic drinks, fresh juices.

House wine from £2.85 glass, £11 bottle. Lager and cider from £2.10.

Children welcome, high chairs, baby change. No dogs. Cash only, cashpoint nearby.

Biederbeckes

Omnivorous bistro

167 Brook St, Dundee, Angus DD1 5BJ
Tel: 01382-229 440
Open: Tue–Sat 12.00–22.30
www.biederbeckesbistro.co.uk

A Bavarian–style jazz bistro with a "foot stomping atmosphere", German lagers and a few vegetarian options. The evening main meals all contain cheese and cream with the exception of a Tampa Bay pakora stir fry £8.95. Vegan "Suzanne Vega" mushroom and onion burger available during the daytime £5.45. Side orders like onion rings, chilli pakora and fries around £2–4.

Lots of soft drinks, like ginger beer and orange juice £1.25–3. Tea and coffee around £2. Beers and wines £3–4. Visa, MC.

Cafe Buongiorno

Omnivorous Italian restaurant

11Bank Street, Dundee, Angus DD1 1RL
Tel: 01382-221 179
Open: Mon & Tue 9.00–18.00, Wed–Sat 9.00–late. Closed Sun. (Phone before travelling any distance, as they sometimes open late or close early.)
www.letseat.at/cafebuongiorno

Italian cafe by day and restaurant by night. All food is made to order and they say they can cater for allergies, religious restrictions and vegans.

Lots of sandwiches including grilled vegetable, onion, tomato and garlic on sesame bread £5.80. Side orders such as oregano wedges; leaf salad; and olives £1.50–3.65. Bean stew with garlic bread, £6.50, can be made without mozzerella.

Children welcome, high chairs. All cards accepted.

Chambers Coffee House

Omnivorous cafe

34 South Tay St, Dundee, Angus DD1 1PD
Tel: 01382-201 533
Open: Mon–Wed 8.00–16.30, Thur–Fri 8.00–late, sat 10.00–late, Sun 11.00–16.30
www.chamberscoffeehouse.co.uk

A cafe with a huge menu containing a variety of vegetarian options. Most are cheesey, but they have chargrilled aubergine and hummus wrap £4.80; garden salad £2.60; vegetable skewers with spicy tomato sauce £7.25; and Moroccan mushrooms with spicy couscous £7.25. Variety of cakes and flapjacks, plus fruit salad £3–4.

Teas and fairtrade coffees £2–3. No soya milk. Large range of alcohol. Children's menu, though it's meaty. Visa, MC.

Dil'Se

Omnivorous Indian restaurant

99–101 Perth Road, Dundee, Angus DD1 4HZ
Tel: 01382-221 501
Open: Mon–Sat 12.00–14.30, 17.00–23.00
www.dilse-restaurant.co.uk
Facebook: Dil'se Restaurant

Modern, upmarket Indian/Bangladeshi with a smaller vegetarian menu than most, but the staff are helpful and can adapt dishes. Vegetarian options are cooked in vegetable oil rather than ghee and can be made vegan on request.

Range of curries £8.95, including dhansaak, rogan josh and pathia. Vegetable thali £13.95. Rice £2.95; vegetable side dishes £2–4.

All cards accepted except Diners.

Other cafes with soya milk with coffee are Caffe Nero, Debenhams or Marks & Spencer.

The Health Store

Vegetarian health food shop

95 Commercial St, Dundee, Angus DD1 2AF
Tel: 01382-201 660
Open: Mon-Sat 9.00-17.30, Sun closed
www.dundeehealthstore.co.uk

Fridge and freezer with soya yogurt, non-dairy cheeses, meat substitutes, pasties, salads, sandwiches, vegan ice-cream by Swedish Glace, Booja Booja, Tofutti. Vegan chocolate by Organica, Plamil, Divine, Montezuma, Booja Booja. Bodycare by Jason, Barefoot Botanicals, Weleda, Avalon, Dr Hauschka, Natracare, Weleda Baby.

Supplements and sports nutrition by all the main brands. Weleda and Nelsons homeopathy, remedies, essential oils. Cleaning by Ecover and refills, Faith in Nature Clear Spring. Some books magazines. MC, Visa.

Betty's Bakehouse

Vegan caterer

Tel: 07515 949 174
www.bettysbakehouse.co.uk
Facebook: Betty's Bakehouse
info@bettysbakehouse.co.uk

Vegan cookies and cupcakes, delivered in Dundee and beyond. Big range of very sexy flavours in two sizes. Most have gluten-free options. Flavours include vanilla; coconut lime; banoffee; mocha; cookie dough; and chocolate mint. Typically £1.30-2. Order through the website and give her three days' notice, as products are baked to order.

Springers Coffee Lounge

Omnivorous cafe & deli

93-97 Castle Street, Forfar, Angus DD8 3AH
Tel: 07541 442556
Open: Mon - Sat 10-18.00
www.forfarcafe.com
Facebook: Springers Coffee Lounge

A very small cafe with a Mediterranean light meal menu. Most of the vegetarian options are cheesy, but they have soup; Greek platter with olives, hummus, dolmas, salad and bread; hummus sandwich with salad; and bruschetta with tomatoes and olive oil. Everything is £4-5.

Coffee, latte, cappuccino £1.50-£2, add 35-50p for soya milk. Tea £1.30.

No cards; cash and cheque only.

They charge for tap water and donate the money to a cancer research charity. Also Priestley's Artisan Chocolates for sale on site; most contain cream, but there's a range of fruit ganaches.

Naturelle

Health food shop

59 Castle Street, Forfar, Angus DD8 3AG
Tel: 01307-468 738
Open: Mon-Sat 9.00-17.00, Sun closed

Lots of gluten-free/coeliac foods. Fridge with tofu, vegetarian sausages, vegan cheeses, falafels, ready meals, veggie haggis. No freezer. Vegan chocolate by Organica, Plamil, Montezuma.

Bodycare by Faith in Nature, Green People, Jason, Tisserand, Natracare, Weleda Baby.

Supplements by Solgar, Vogel, Quest, Nature's Aid and lots more. Nelsons, New Era and Helios homeopathy, Balance Scottish essential oils. Therapy room upstairs with Swedish and

aromatherapy massage, reflexology, Reiki, food intolerance testing.
Cleaning by Ecover, BioD. Gifts such as candles, incense, jewellery, cards.
MC, Visa. Gift vouchers. Postal service.

Angus chain stores

Holland & Barrett, Angus

Health food shops

229 High Street, **Arbroath**, Angus DD11 1DZ
Tel: 01241–434 565
Open: Mon–Sat 9.00–17.30, Sun closed

Unit 20, Wellgate Centre, **Dundee**, Angus DD1 2AU. Tel: 01382–205 726
Open: Mon–Sat 9.00–17.30, Sun 12–16.00

Argyll

Ford House

Omnivorous guest house

Ford, **Lochgilphead**, Argyll PA31 8RH
Tel: 0845-456 1208. Mobile 07789 388 146.
International: +44-1546-810 273.
Open: Easter–October, plus often in winter;
check when enquiring.
www.ford-house.com/home.htm

A grand old 3 star guest house in a stunning location surrounded by hills, forests and lochs. Not easily accessible by public transport and they don't do evening meals, so you'll need a car. Loch Lomond is a short drive away.
Several rooms and a log cabin, from £30 adult, £20 child. The family suite is two adjoining rooms with a private bathroom that accommodates 5–6.
A typical fried breakfast will include Linda McCartney vegan sausages, plus beans on toast and tomatoes. Soya milk and gluten-free bread available on request when booking.
Children of all ages welcome. No dogs. No smoking anywhere in the house. Eco-friendly cleaning products used. Cash and cheque only.

Eco Grain & Health Store

Wholefood shop

50 Hillfoot Street, **Dunoon,** Argyll PA23 7DT
Tel: 01369-705 106
Open: Sat–Wed 9.00–17.30,
Thu–Fri 9.00–18.00, Sun closed.

Well-stocked wholefood shop that sells fruit and vegetables, packaged and tinned wholefoods, vegan chocolate and flapjacks. Fridge and freezer with Bute Island dairy-free cheeses, various meat-free products, tofu etc.
Bodycare by Jason, Faith in Nature and Weleda. Cleaning products by Method and Ecover, some refills available. Aromatherapy oils, supplements and homeopathy.
Therapy room at the back offers reflexology, massage, craniosacral therapy, aromatherapy and Reiki. Visa, MC.

The Quaich

Village shop with wholefoods

Kimelford, by Oban, Argyll PA34 4XA
Tel: 01852-200 271
Open: Mon–Wed 9.00–17.30, Thu–Sat 9.00–21.00, Sun 10.00–13.00 (Post Office has shorter hours)
www.thequaich.net

This is a grocery shop, craft shop, off-licence, post office, Tourist Information Centre, bank and cafe all rolled into one. The cafe has virtually nothing vegetarian, but the shop stocks a range of wholefoods and organic products, wine, fruit and vegetables.

The Smiddy

Omnivorous cafe

Smithy Lane, **Lochgilphead,** Argyll PA31 8TA
Tel: 01546–603 606
Open: Mon–Sat 10–17.00 (last orders 16.00)

A cosy little cafe tucked away down an alley. Daily-changing main meals around £7 with plenty of choice for us, including veggieburgers; baked potatoes; bean chilli; and loads of salads. Always vegan options.
Very family-friendly, usually full of kids. MC, Visa.

Cockles Fine Foods

Grocery and wholefood shop

11 Argyll Street, **Lochgilphead**, PA31 8LZ
Tel: 01546-606 292
Open: Mon to Fri 9.30–17.30
Saturday 9.30–17.00 (Closed for lunch each day 12.45–13.15)
www.cocklesfinefoods.com

This shop is packed with quality foods and ingredients, such as jams, chutneys, local bread and coffees. In addition to meat and fish, they have a large range of wholefoods such as yeast paté, dried fruit, nuts and seeds, plus a fridge and freezer with smoked tofu, vegan cheese and vegan ice cream. The friendly owner is happy to slice bread for you if you're going on a picnic and to get extra products in stock.
No alcohol licence. Visa, MC.

Cafe Barge

Omnivorous cafe

Harbour St, Tarbert PA29 6UD
Tel: 07949 723 128
Open: usually Mon–Sat 9.00–18.00
(Can get booked for wedding receptions and sometimes closes for a few weeks in winter, so phone before travelling)
www.cafebarge.co.uk

A half vegetarian, half fish cafe on a Dutch barge in Tarbert Harbour, Loch Fyne. Lots of tapas style dishes. There are no main meals or starters as such; you just combine dishes according to your appetite. A vegan meal could typically be hummus with oatcakes; potatoes in hot tomato sauce; and pine nuts, spinach and sultanas fried in olive oil. Expect to pay around £12 a head for a full meal or £4 for a snack.
Bread and cakes supplied by Tapa Bakehouse in Glasgow.
Serves Vintage Roots organic vegetarian wines, around £3.50–4 a glass. Bottled beers and cider £3.15.
Well-behaved children welcome, though not suitable for pushchairs. Children's portions. Note no wheelchair access. No smoking anywhere on the boat. MC, Visa.

SCOTLAND Argyll

Itadaki Zen vegan Japanese restaurant, Oban

Itadaki Zen, Oban

Vegan Japanese restaurant

Craigard Road, Oban PA34 5NP
Tel: 01631-565 942
Open: Mon–Sat 17.30–21.30, Sun closed;
Dec–Mar also closed Wed; Feb closed all month
www.itadakizen.com

Banzai! This elegant and authentically Japanese vegan restaurant opened in October 2011, sister to their first one in Kings Cross, London, where you could dine before catching a train to Scotland.

Sushi are their speciality. The top of the range myaku sushi rice is made with organic brown rice flour to compensate for the shortcomings of white rice, plus egoma wild sesame oil, then combined with organic vegetables, seaweeds and wild plants. 6 pieces for £7, medium 8 £8.50, large 12 £12.50. Regular sushi £2.90 for 3, with seaweeds, shiitake mushrooms and other seasonal vegetables, £5.50 for 6.

Chapche £7.50 sweet potato starch noodles cooked with vegetables, kikurage mushrooms and shiitake. Harumaki deep-fried or grilled spring rolls, 2 for £3.50, 4 £6, 8 £10. Udon noodles in miso sauce with veg £8. Seaweeds udon £7 with okara (byproduct of making soya milk), peanuts, seaweed and egoma wild sesame oil.

Crispy kakiage tempura £2 made with deep fried carrots, onions and seaweeds, medium £6.50, large £7.50. Green salad £3.50. Ryokusaimaki lightly cooked greens enfolding tofu and veg £3.50–£6. Tofu £3, grilled tofu steak £3.90, miso soup £2, seaweeds nimono £3. Pickles £1.

Dinner set £12 with 6 sushi, miso soup, 2 deep-fried or grilled spring rolls, 2

crispy veg tempura. Kimpab Chapche set £18 with chapche veg noodles, 8 pieces of kimpab style sushi, 2 spring rolls or tofu, miso soup.

Sugar-free desserts £3–4.50 are muffins, soya milk kanten jelly pudding with azki beans, white sesame kanten pudding, pudding of the day.

Organic juices £2.50. Caffeine-free Oriental coffee £2. Sasou tea £2 with sasa bamboo leaf and soba buckwheat seeds. Blended grain tea £3.10 with soya milk, jujube, pumpkin powder, pine nuts and black sesame.

All alcohol is organic. Hyakusa-sai sake rice wine with 10 Oriental herbs £9.50 for 180ml jar, £35 bottle. Wines from £4 glass, £13.90 bottle. Beers £3.70 bottle. 10% evening service charge.

Children welcome, baby chair.

No dogs. MC, Visa; cashpoint nearby.

The Coriander

Omnivorous Indian restaurant

8 Soroba Road, Oban PA34 4HU
Tel: 01631-570 806
Open: Every day 11.30–14.00, 17.00–23.00
www.thecoriander.co.uk

A new Indian restaurant with a slightly more varied menu than the others in town. Lunch menu options include stir-fried vegetable and herb sandwich for £4. Starters cost around £3 and include chickpea chaat on flatbread; samosas; and pakoras. There are also a few curries.

The evening menu has the same starters and a larger range of curries for around £7. Vegetarian menu has around 10 choices. Rice £1.85.

Children's portions available. Not licensed, but you bring your own alcohol from Tesco next door. MC, Visa.

Julie's Coffee House

Omnivorous cafe

33 Stafford St, Oban PA34 5NH
Tel: 01631–565 952
Open: Tue–Sat 10.00–17.00, plus Mondays
during Jul–Aug

A small, welcoming cafe right next to the distillery and a few minutes walk from the ferry terminal. Serves baked potatoes, sandwiches, soup, salads and cakes. There are always vegetarian options, though vegan choices are more limited. Everything is made to order, so dishes can be adapted. Soup (usually veggie) with bread £4, ciabattas around £5 and a full meal £7.

They have soya milk. Children are welcome and there's a booster chair. Outside tables, where smoking and dogs are allowed. Visa, MC.

Millstone Wholefoods

Vegetarian wholefood shop

15 High Street, Oban PA34 4BG
Tel: 01631–562 704
Open: Mon–Sat 9.15–17.15, Sun closed
www.millstonewholefoods.co.uk
contact@millstonewholefoods.co.uk

Oban is the gateway to the Isles, with ferries to Mull for Iona, Isla, Collinsee, Coll and beyond. Since 1978, people going self-catering have been stocking up here, the only wholefood shop in the region, and islanders buy in bulk such as sacks of flour. You can email before arrival and they'll get your order ready.

Lots of organic produce such as fruit and veg. Bread delivered on Wednesday. Fridge and freezer with vegan cheeses, vegetarian haggis, sausages, Cheatin' ham, lots of tofus and pates, seitan, vegan yogurt, vegan ice-cream by Booja Booja and Swedish Glace.

Vegan chocolate by Plamil, Booja Booja, Vivani, Montezuma.

Bodycare by Weleda, Barefoot Botanicals, Green People, Tisserand, Faith in Nature, Yaoh, Natracare, Weleda baby. Supplements by Solgar, FSC, Quest, Nature's Own, Nature's Aid, Vogel. Nelsons and Weleda homeopathy, Absolute Aromas essential oils.

Cleaning by Ecover. Health, New Age and cookery books, magazines, cards, candles, incense, salt lamps, meditation and relaxation CDs. MC, Visa.

Nearby is **The Therapy Rooms** at 26 High Street with massage including shiatsu, aromatherapy, deep tissue, cranio-sacral, Bowen. 01866–844 088.

Ayrshire

Ayr restaurants

Su Casa

Omnivorous cafe with evening events

115 High Street, **Ayr** KA7 1QL
Tel: 01292– 618 657
Open: Mon–Sat 9–18.00, Sun 11–18.00,
plus open some evenings for events
www.sucasaayr.com

A new 75% vegetarian cafe specialising in light meals from around the world and quality ethical coffee roasted on site. Local vegetarians tell us it's great value and good for vegan food.

Expect to pay £4.50–£6 for daily-changing menu items such as falafel platter, chickpea curry, and quesadilla wrap with tomatoes and chutney.

Not many desserts at the time of going to print, but they're working on that and bringing in vegan ones.

Organic teas, coffees and canned drinks £1.75–2. They have soya milk. Bring your own alcohol.

Children welcome, high chairs. Portion size can be adapted for children.

Acoustic sets every Thursday from 8pm, £5 entry. Often comedy nights. Sometimes closed in the evenings for private banquets, so phone in advance if travelling any distance.

Ayrshire shops

Jan de Vries, Largs

Health food shop

1 Tron Place, **Largs,** North Ayrshire, KA30 8AR
Tel: 01475–689 123
Open: Mon–Fri 9.30–17.30, Sat 9.30–17.00
Sun closed
www.jandevrieshealth.co.uk

Large range of wholefoods, specialising in gluten-free products such as bread. Fridge and freezer with Bute Island and Tofutti vegan cheeses, vegan gourmet pate, and meat substitutes. They stock Swedish Glace ice-cream and Booja Booja can be ordered in. Plamil and Xylitol chocolate, with Booja Booja at Christmas.

Bodycare includes Faith in Nature, Dead Sea Magik, Avalon, Barefoot Botanicals Jason, Weleda, Green People, Napiers; Weleda and Green People Baby.

Cleaning products include Method with washing up refills, Ecover, Ecozone, and Living Naturally.

Supplements include Solgar, Nature's Aid, Weleda, Vogel. Weleda homeopathy, Jan de Vries remedies. Natural by Nature essential oils. Food allergy testing, Jan de Vries occasionally in shop. Stocks Jan de Vries books.

Anything else can be ordered in if you phone ahead (phone by Mon for Tues delivery). MC, Visa.

Jan de Vries, Prestwick

Health food shop

33 Main Street, **Prestwick** KA9 1AD
Tel: 01292-471429
Open: Mon–Sat 9.00–17.00, Sun closed
www.jandevrieshealth.co.uk

A small shop specialising in health foods, supplements and vitamins. No fridge or freezer or takeaway food. Sells a small amount of vegan chocolate, mostly Green and Blacks.
Bodycare includesTisserand, Faith in Nature, Weleda, Natracare, Weleda baby.
Supplements include Solgar, Lamberts, Nature's Aid, Weleda, Jan de Vries range. Weleda and New Era homeopathy. Essential oils.
Cleaning products by Ecover with hand soap refills, Method. Jan de Vries books. MC, Visa.
Anything else can be ordered in if you phone ahead (phone by Mon for Tues delivery)
#owner Jeanette, Liz managers
Most places to eat out in Prestwick have vegetarian options.

Jan de Vries, Troon

Health food shop

6 Church Street, **Troon** KA10 6AU
Tel: 01292-310344
Open: Mon–Sat 9.00–17.00, Mon and Fri from 9.30, Sun closed
www.jandevrieshealth.co.uk

A small shop with no fridge or freezer. Vegan chocolate by Plamil, Booja Booja, flapjacks and bars.
Bodycare by Barefoot Botanicals, Dr Hauschka, Weleda, Natracare, Weleda Baby.
Supplements by Solgar, Quest, Nature's Aid, Optima, Better You, Optivac. Homeopathy and remedies by Vogel

and Jan de Vries. A few essential oils. Cleaning by Ecover and Method.
Free magazines. They can order in anything else if you tell them before before Monday 9am to collect on Tue afternoon or Wed morning. MC, Visa.

Holland & Barrett, Ayrshire

Health food shops

155 High Street, **Ayr**, Ayrshire KA7 1QW
Tel: 01292 284895
Open: Mon–Sat 9.00–17.30, Sun 12–17.00

11 Rivergate, **Irvine**, Ayrshire KA12 8EH
Tel: 01294 278815
Open: Mon–Sat 09.00–17.30, Sun 12–16.00

6 The Cross, **Kilmarnock**, Ayrshire KA1 1DH
Tel: 01563–574304
Open: Mon–Sat 09.00–17.30, Sun closed

29 Nelson Street, **Largs**, Ayrshire KA30 8LN
Tel: 01475 686167
Open: Mon–Sat 09.00–17.30, Sun closed

23 Portland Street, **Troon**, South Ayrshire KA10 6AA. Tel: 01292–312919
Open: Mon–Sat 9.00–17.30, Sun closed

Borders

Borders – Eyemouth

Giacopazzi's

Italian chippie and ice-cream parlour

20 Harbour Road, Eyemouth TD14 5HU
Tel: 01890–750317
Open: Sun–Thu 9.00–20.00, Fri–Sat –20.30
www.giacopazzis.co.uk

Traditional Italian family run ice-cream parlour, chip shop and pizzeria. They have 3 to 5 vegan sorbets on offer every day, though the choice of veggie savoury food is very limited, with the chips being fried in beef dripping.
Children's meals, high chair. Outdoor seating.

Borders – Galashiels

Moondogs

Omnivorous coffee shop & art gallery

6 Channel Street, Galashiels TD1 1BA
Tel: 01896–758 454
Open: Mon–Sat 9.30–18.00, Sun closed, monthly live music Sat till 23.00
www.moondogcafe.co.uk
www.facebook.com/pages/
  Moondogs/15925707973

Independent coffee shop and art gallery with locally sourced, ethically produced products; relocated from Reading where it was popular with local vegans.
Falafel wraps are vegan £5.50. Cakes include vegan brownies £2. Edinburgh Artisan Roasters coffee, latte, cappuccino, mocha £1.80–2.50; they have soya milk. Juices £1.80.
Ticket-only music nights with top musicians, bring your own bottle, £15 includes any food from the menu and cover charge for the band. Regular "Stitch and Bitch" open craft group on a Sunday, ask for details.
Art and craft in the shop is generally sourced locally though they do have from other areas. Jewellery, pottery,

photography.
Children welcome, toys, games, high chair. Outside seating, dogs welcome there. MC, Visa.

Borders – Kelso

Kelso Wholefoods

Wholefood shop

54 Woodmarket, Kelso TD5 7AX
Tel: 01573–225 664
Open: Mon–Sat 9.00–17.00, Sun closed
www.kelsowholefoods.co.uk
www.kelso.bordernet.co.uk

Small shop with lots of gluten/wheat- and dairy-free, herbs and spices. Local seasonal organic veg. Fridge and freezer with vegan cheese by Tofutti, Bute Island Scheese and Redwood, tofu, Provamel soya yogurt, Swedish Glace.
Vegan chocolate by Moo Free, Montezuma.
Bodycare by Faith in Nature. Ecover cleaning products. MC, Visa over £10.

Chain stores

Holland & Barrett, Galashiels

Health food shops

Unit 3 Douglas Bridge, **Galashiels**, Selkirkshire TD1 1BH. Tel: 01896–7542 56
Open: Mon–Sat 9.00–17.30, Sun 12–16.00

Here are some places just over the border in Northumberland, from the book *Vegetarian North of England*.

The Coach House

Omnivorous guest house

Crookham, Cornhill-on-Tweed TD12 4TD.
(on A697, 1 hour drive from Edinburgh or Newcastle)
Tel: 01890-820293
Open: Feb-Nov
www.coachhousecrookham.com

A complex of renovated old farm buildings, including a 1680s cottage and an old smithy, surrounding a sun-trap courtyard. 3 traditional and 7 modern rooms including disabled, all ensuite or with own bathroom, £39-55 per person, single occupancy £15-35 extra. Beware of leather furniture in most rooms. Vegetarian and vegan cooked breakfasts. Dinner £22.95. Dogs welcome in certain rooms. Visa, MC +2%, no charge for debit cards.

Kielder Youth Hostel

4 star youth hostel

YHA Kielder, Butteryhaugh, Kielder Village, Hexham NE48 1HQ
Tel: 01434-250 195
Open: all year, 24 hour access
Reception 09.00-10.00, 17.00-21.00
www.yha.org.uk
Email: kielder@yha.org.uk

Kielder is the most remote village in England, great for cycling, walking, wildlife and watersports. There is a village store with banking facilities open normal shop hours. Secure bike storage. Laundry. The nearest super-market and bank are 17 miles away.
May-Oct adult £20 each in a twin bed room (two of those), £14 winter. Single-sex dorm £18 summer, winter £16.40, under-18 £13.50/£12. Non-YHA members pay £3 extra (U-18 £1.50), and two people at the same address can join for £22.95 so if you stay at more than 3 hostels a year it is worth it.
This hostel sometimes only accepts group bookings in winter months.
Buffet breakfast £4.95 with plenty of hot and cold choices, good for vegetarians, if vegan check when booking.
Evening meal starters £2.50-3.50, mains £5.50-6.95, always has a vege-tarian choice, vegan if you warn them, such as courgette curry with coconut milk with rice and popadoms; lots of bean dishes such as 3-bean casserole or chilli. Kids' portions. Beer (Wylan Brewery, vegan) and wine available. No dogs. Children welcome, 2 carrycots. MC, Visa.

Noah's Place

Omnivorous organic B&B

31 Main Street, Spittal, Berwick upon Tweed, Northumberland TD15 1QY
Tel: 01289-332 141
Open mainly Easter and summer
www.noahsplace.co.uk

Family-run B&B in a house built in 1792 on a Georgian high street, near sandy Spittal beach in the historic fortified border town of Berwick-upon-Tweed.
One room has a kingsize bed and a bunk bed, the other has a king size and a single. £25 per adult; under-13 £12.50, under-4 free. Extra Z-bed £15. Free cot. Single occupant £30.
Cotton pillows and duvets with duck/goose feather filling. Bicycle storage. Mainly open Easter and summer because of long-term residents, check website. No dogs. Cash or cheque only.

Ravensdowne Guest House

Omnivorous guest house

40 Ravensdowne, **Berwick–upon–Tweed**,
Northumberland TD15 1DQ
Tel: 01289-306 992
Open: all year except 24–27 Dec
Station: Berwick 7mins walk
www.40ravensdowne.co.uk

1760 townhouse in the centre of
Berwick near the Elizabethan fortified
walls. 2 double (one with 4–poster), 1
twin, £30–40 per person, 1 single £35–
50, all ensuite. Full English veggie
breakfast. The owners have a vegan
sister and vegetarian daughter. 3–
course evening meals £10–15 include
veggie pie, Indian, Indonesian style Thai,
vegan, coeliac and nut–free on request.
They can recommend cafes for lunch.
Free on street parking. Secure covered
bike storage. Free wifi. Totally non-
smoking. No children under 12. No
pets. MC, Visa.

Cafe Curio

Omnivorous French bistro–cafe

52 Bridge Street, Berwick TD15 1AQ
Tel: 01289-302 666
Open: Mon–Sat 10.00–16.00 or later,
Fri–Sat dinners by reservation, Sun closed

Eating out in Berwick can seem grim but
this very unusual cafe has regular local
vegan and vegetarian customers,
knows what we like and has gluten–free
options. The American chef uses local
ingredients with a French colonial twist,
such as potato and butterbean soup.
Always a vegetarian option £5.95–8.95
on the menu and they try to avoid
basing it on cheese, e.g. stuffed peppers
with couscous and pine nuts, rice
noodles with veg stock, poached Asian

veg with mirin glaze, and for dessert
they could make you poached plums
with almonds. Sometimes open Fri–Sat
night if you book, £25 for 4 courses,
either a fixed menu or as a taster menu.
Pot of tea or bottomless cup of coffee
£2. House wine £3.50 glass, bottles
from £15. Bottled beer £3.
They also sell antiques and in fact
everything that isn't nailed down is for
sale including the furniture and cutlery,
though you might have to wait for
someone to finish using it. Children
welcome, high chairs. No dogs. Cash or
cheque only, cashpoints nearby.

Sinners Cafe

Omnivorous cafe

1 Sidey Court, Berwick upon Tweed
TD15 1DR. Tel: 01289-302 621
Winter: Mon–Sat 10.00–15.00, Sun closed.
Summer Mon–Sat 9.00–16.00,
Sun 10.00–15.00.
www.berwickbedandbreakfast.co.uk
/sinners–cafe–bar.htm

Local vegans come here for a great
value cooked breakfast £4.50 including
orange juice or a hot drink. They now
have a vegetarian menu, which includes
panini and toasties; filled baked
potatoes; chilli; dairy–free mushroom
stroganoff; and veggie burger with
chips and salad. Meals typically cost £4–
5. Soup £3. Cakes, tray bakes and
scones now have gluten–free and vegan
options. Tea and coffee £1–1.20; they
have soya milk. Children welcome, high
chair, no big prams inside. Dogs
welcome in the courtyard seating area.
Car park nearby. MC, Visa.

Caffe Nero at 77–79 Marygate is the
only other cafe we know of to do soya
milk, though it's 30p extra. Open: Mon–
Sat 9.00–18.00, Sun 9.00–18.00.

The Green Shop

Omnivorous organic food & eco shop

30 Bridge Street, Berwick upon Tweed
TD15 1AQ. Tel: 01289-305 566
Open: Mon–Sat 9.00–17.30, Sun closed
www.berwickholidaycottages.co.uk/
  green-shop.htm
www.exploreberwick.co.uk/Stores/
  Green.htm

Family-run business with nothing
tested on animals and locally produced
where possible. Organic fruit and veg,
vegan and veggie foods, beers, wines,
spirits, frozen fruit, seeds, non-dairy
yogurt. Fairtrade snacks. Clothing, cards
and crafts. Toiletries, make-up, sun
cream, essential oils.

The Market Shop

**Vegetarian health food shop & art
gallery**

48 Bridge St, Berwick–upon–Tweed
TD15 1AQ. Tel: 01289-307749
Open: Mon–Sat 9.30–17..00, closed Sun
www.exploreberwick.co.uk/Stores/
  Sallyport.htm

Full range of wholefoods. Lots of
gluten-free. Fridge (but no freezer) with
vegan yogurt and cheeses, hummus.
Huge range of herbs and spices. Lots of
teas. Good for walkers with bars, Plamil
vegan chocolate, nuts, seeds and dried
fruit.
Bodycare by Avalon, full Weleda range
and baby, Thursday Plantation, Dead
Sea Magik. Supplements by Solgar,
Bioforce, Viridian, Weleda. Homeopathy
and remedies, Absolute Aromas
essential oils. Food allergy testing by
appointment. Ecover cleaning products.
Also nautical gifts, art supplies and a
gallery. MC, Visa.

Holland & Barrett, Berwick

Health food shop

74 Marygate, **Berwick** TD15 1BN
Tel: 01289-309262
Open: Mon–Sat 9.00–17.30, Sun 11–16.00

Dumfries & Galloway

Purelands Retreat Centre & Tibetan Tea Rooms

Buddhist Monastery & Tibetan Centre, vegetarian cafe & accommodation

Kagyu Samye Ling, Eskdalemuir, Langholm, Dumfriesshire DG13 0QL
Tel: 013873-732 32
Open: All year, every day 9.00–17.00 (can close half an hour early on quiet days)
Train: Lockerbie 15 miles then bus 112 or taxi
www.samyeling.org

This was the first Tibetan Buddhist centre established in the west, in 1967. Day visitors are welcome – you can stroll around the peace garden and grounds, relax in the Tibetan tea rooms, browse in the shop and meditate in the temple, which opens early in the morning. If you want to sit with the monks and nuns, the best time to arrive is early afternoon.

The **Tibetan Tea Rooms** is completely vegetarian and they have soya milk, though almost all of the food contains dairy products. Light meals include soup, paninis and pasties. Range of teas including Choco Aztec spice tea.

No alcohol allowed on site. Children welcome, but no high chairs. No dogs. There's a smoking area in the garden.

Accommodation available for adults only. Dormitory £24 per person, twin £28.50, single £37, camping £15.

They run weekend workshops, retreats and day classes. Self-catering family accommodation nearby in Eskdalemuir.

Sunrise Wholefoods

Wholefood shop

49 King Street, Castle Douglas, Kirkcudbrightshire DG7 1AE
Tel: 01556–504 455
Open: Mon–Sat 9.30–17.00

A very well-stocked shop specialising in wholefood ingredients: they claim to have the largest range of herbs and spices in Scotland, plus nuts, dried fruit and other wholefoods.

Fruit and vegetables, bread (including gluten-free), and vegan takeaway pasties and tarts. Fridge with meat substitutes, tofu and dairy-free desserts and cheeses. Freezer with dairy-free ice cream.

Flapjacks, energy bars and chocolate, including Booja Booja and Montezuma. Organic wines.

Bodycare by Faith in Nature and Weleda. Cleaning by Ecover and Bio D. Natracare women's products.

Supplements, vitamins, Bach flower remedies, homeopathy, remedies and essential oils.

Small range of books about green issues.

Steiner Community

Omnivorous farm shop & cafe

Loch Arthur, Beeswing, Dumfries, DG2 8JQ
(just off A711 south-west of Dumfries)
Tel: 01387-760 296
www.locharthur.org.uk

Loch Arthur is a community for men
and women with learning disabilities,
run on Steiner principles. They sell dried
wholefoods in their farm shop, plus
organic vegetables and chutneys. Their
pies all contain butter. Also sell meat
from cattle slaughtered on site.
They plan to open a cafe summer 2012,
which will have vegetarian options.

Jan de Vries, Dumfries

Health food shop

10 Church Crescent, **Dumfries** DG1 1DF
Tel: 01387-270760
Open: Mon–Fri 9.00 -17.15, Sat 9.00-17.00
Sun closed
www.jandevrieshealth.co.uk

A small shop in the Jan de Vries chain
that specialises in supplements. Stocks
local breads, including gluten-free.
No fridge, freezer or takeaway food.
Dairy-free chocolate and flapjacks,
including Ma Baker range.
Bodycare by Faith in Nature and Weleda.
Natracare women's products. Ecover
cleaning products. Supplements by Jan
de Vries, Vogel, Lifeplan and Weleda.
Homeopathy. Essential oils. Stocks the
full range of Jan de Vries books.
Friendly, helpful staff, who are happy to
order in other products on request.

The Green Tea House

Omnivorous tea rooms

The Old Bank, Chapel Street, **Moniaive**,
Dumfries & Galloway DG3 4EJ
Tel: 01848-200 099
Open: Apr–Nov, Every day 11–17.00, Nov–
Apr 11–16.00. Evening bistro during summer
months: 18.00–21.00
www.green_teahouse.co.uk
www.moniaive.org.uk (local events)

Moniaive is a small but well-equipped
village full of artists and folk musicians.
It has a post office, pub, grocery, petrol
station, car park and this cafe, which is
mostly organic, specialises in dietery
sensitivities and has lots of vegetarian
options.
Light meals £3.20–6.50 include
aubergine and tomato bake; toasties
and Tofutti cream cheese bagels;
locally-made vegan haggis; and sweet
potato and cashew tatin. Always 4–5
vegetarian soups, of which almost all
are dairy-free. Vegan desserts (£2–3)
include chocolate gluten-free brownies;
and date and apple slice.
Fairtrade, organic drinks. Pint of tea £1;
coffee £2–3; and juices £1.50. Not
licensed, though you can bring your
own. Pets welcome. Children welcome,
high chairs. Now takes all cards. Garden
with outside seating. Monthly themed
nights with many small courses from
one country £25 per head, see website.
Moniaive has lots of local arts and crafts,
with special events all year including a
big folk festival in May, with temporary
camping.

Jan de Vries, Stranraer

Health food shop

52 Hanover Street, **Stranraer** DG9 7RP
Tel: 01776-704702
Open: Mon-Sat 9.00-17.00, Sun closed
www.jandevrieshealth.co.uk

This shop has a fridge with tofu, Provamel yoghurts and Bute Island vegan cheeses. The small freezer has some Redwoods Rashers and other meat substitutes and they can get ice cream in to order. Good range of Plamil and Vivali organic chocolate, energy bars and some flapjacks.

Bodycare brands include Weleda, Dead Sea Magik, Aqua Oleum and Tisserand. Natracare, Weleda Baby. Ecover, Faith in Nature and Method cleaning products.

Supplements include Lifeplan, Nature's Aid, Solgar and Quest. Vogel specialist, with their entire range.

Aqua Oleum essential oils.

There's a clinic offering Podiatry, Indian Head Massage, Food Intolerance testing and homeopathy.

Jan de Vries books, vegan and allergy-friendly cookbooks.

All cards accepted. The staff are very knowledgable and happy to advise. They can order products in for you.

Holland & Barrett, Dumfries

Health food shops

Unit 16, The Lorebourne Shopping Centre
Dumfries DG1 2BD. Tel: 01387-253 551
Open: Mon-Sat 9.00-17.30, Sun 12-16.00

Unit 12 Gretna Gateway Outlet Village, Glasgow Rd, **Gretna**, Dumfriesshire DG16 5GG. Tel: 01461-337 256
Open: Mon-Sun 10.00-18.00

Fife

Cleveden House

Omnivorous guest house

3 Murray Place, **St Andrews** KY16 9AP
Tel: 01334–474 212
www.clevedenhouse.co.uk

Family-owned four star guest house in the heart of St Andrews, near the centre, university, sandy beaches and the famous Old Course.

Six ensuite rooms: 1 single, 2 double, 1 twin, 2 double/twin. Rooms have hairdryer, tv, hospitality tray, internet access.

Vegetarian and vegan breakfasts include hot dishes cooked to order. Smoking allowed in private courtyard.

This is the only guest house we found that specifically advertises its vegetarian and vegan offerings. We did call to enquire about prices in November 2011 and offered the owner a free listing, but he told us he was not interested and hung up, perhaps after bad experiences with other guides that charge a fortune for listings. Hopefully you will have a better experience!

Pillars of Hercules

Vegetarian organic cafe, omnivorous farm shop & camping

Pillars of Hercules Farm, Falkland, Cupar KY15 7AD
Tel: 01337–857 749 (but they prefer you to email, especially about accommodation)
Cafe open: every day 10.00–17.00
plus monthly evening restaurant
Shop open: Every day 9.00–18.00
Closed 25–26 Dec, 1–2 Jan
www.pillars.co.uk

Expanding organic fruit and veg farm plus native trees and free-range hens.

There's a vegetarian, organic cafe on site, which becomes a much more expensive omnivorous restaurant once a month (see website). The cafe does soups, salads, toasties, occasionally a vegan special, and cakes including vegan choc cherry and gingerbread. Besides the soups, the vegan options are limited, though they can do a hummus and chutney sandwich. Prices range from £3–5. Bread baked on site. They have oatcakes and rice cakes as wheat-free options.

Children welcome, high chairs. Outside seating area, where you can smoke and take dogs.

There's also a wholefood shop, which sells everything from breakfast cereals to wine, and the "Best selection of organic fruit and vegetables north of the Forth." Plenty of vegan products such as soya cheese, beers, wines and champagne, though they also sell venison and salmon.

If you want to stay, they have a campsite (£5), bunk barn and bothy (a rustic cottage with basic facilities and a wood stove). Enquire about price of bothy as it varies.

Note that free range chickens and turkeys are raised for slaughter on the farm.

Cafe Moka

Omnivorous cafe

29 Bonnygate, Cupar, Fife KY15 4BU
Tel: 01334–650 505
Open: Mon to Sat 9.30–16.00 (but flexible – if they see people waiting outside, they'll open early and they won't usher you out)

This cafe has a veggie chef and plenty of menu options for us, including spinach and chickpea burger, hummus and roast veg paninis, mushroom pate, and bakes. The soups are vegetarian and they always have vegan and gluten-free options, including cakes and usually sticky toffee pudding – this is the only place in Cupar town centre where vegans are well catered for. Meals cost from £3 for a snack to £6.50 for a big plateful with side salads. Food is made on site. Hot drinks £1.85–2.20

If you're vegan or gluten-free and phone to say you're coming, they'll make the selection of food larger.

They have soya milk and dairy-free margarine. Children's menu and high chairs. There's a bookshop above and a garden round the back where you can smoke and take dogs. MC, Visa.

Veggie Fife meet here regularly.

Kirkcaldy

Health Food and More

Health food shop & herbal medicine

132 St. Clair Street, Kirkcaldy KY1 2BZ
Tel: 01592–566 446
Open: Tue–Sat 9.30–17.30, Sun–Mon closed
www.healthfoodandherbal.co.uk

Lots of wheat, gluten and dairy-free products. Local bread. Fridge with Redwood, Vegideli, Tofutti, Taifun, hummus, Delphi pot salads such as couscous, lentil salad, chickpea salad. Frozen Clive's pies, Swedish Glace, Booja

Booja, Freedom vegan frozen dessert.

Vegan chocolate by Moo Free, Plamil, Booja Booja.

IOrganic skincare products by Dr Hauschka, Lavera, Faith in Nature, Rosa Mesquita, Flexitol, Eco Bath, Jason, Giovanni.

Supplements by Bioforce, Solgar, Viridian, Nature's Aid, FSC, Higher Nature, Biohealth, Lifeplan, Pharmanord, Biocare, Pukka, Optibac.

Herbal and homeopathic remedies by Weleda and some Helios, dried herbs, Bach Flower. In-house medical herbalist, herbal dispensary and clinic. Essential oils.

They can order in anything else you need within a week. MC, Visa.

St Andrews restaurants

Nahm-Jim

Omnivorous Thai/Japanese restaurant

60–62 Market St, **St Andrews** KY16 9NT
Tel: 01334–474 000 / 400
Open: Mon–Sun 12.00–16.45, 18.00–24.00, Fri–Sat –01.00
www.nahm-jim.co.uk (menus)

Big, classy Thai restaurant which appeared in *Ramsay's Best Restaurants* in 2010. Ground floor is open all day from 12.00 and upstairs too from 18.00. Prices are higher in the evening. Veggie starters and soups around £4 lunch, £5–£8.50 dinner, such as spring rolls, Thai soups, sweetcorn fritters, gyoza dumplings, tempura, edamame. Miso soup £2.50. Main courses around £9-10 lunch, £10.50-12.50 dinner, such as assorted tempura, stir-fry Thai veg and rice, sweet potato massaman curry and rice, aubergine green curry, sweet and sour tofu with veg, pumpkin croquette katsu curry, and chilli tofu ramen soup. Extra rice £2.50. Bento box lunch £9.95, dinner £12.95.

Desserts £4–7 include mango and sweet coconut rice, or black sticky rice toffee made with coconut milk. Coffee from £1.50.

House wine £3.95 medium glass, £5.25 large, £15.50 bottle. Draught Japanese beer £3.70 pint, bottled Thai beers £3.25. Cocktails £5.95. Sake £8–13 flask, £30–36 bottle.

Pizza Express, St Andrews

Omnivorous Italian restaurant

3–4 Logies Lane, St Andrews KY16 9NL
Tel: 01334–477 109
Open: Sun–Thu 11.30–22.00, Fri–Sat 23.00
www.pizzaexpress.com

For menu see Glasgow. Disabled access. Children welcome, baby changing. Outside seating. Meeting room.

Zest

Omnivorous cafe, coffee & juice bar

95 South Street, St Andrews KY16 9QW
Tel: 01334–471 451
Open: Mon–Sun 08.00–18.00 or a bit earlier if not busy, Sun 08.00–17.00; summer can be open till 19.00 if warm
Facebook: Zest Juice and Coffee Bar

This branch has more food than Zest to Go, though both are good for veggies and vegans. 3 or 4 soups, most are vegan and gluten–free, £2.95 eat in, £2.50 take–away. Sandwiches £2.95 eat in (£2.45 take–away), baguettes £3.95/£3.45, 7 are vegetarian and 2 vegan, such as roasted veg, or beetroot and carrot, sometimes hummus. Soup and sandwich deal £4.95 eat in or take–away. Also bagels, filled baked potatoes £3.35–3.85, gluten–free bread.

More smoothies here and fewer juices than at Zest to Go, but in both branches you can design your own juice cocktail from whatever they have on the day.

Smoothies £2.95 to £4.35. They have soya milk.

Coffee, cappuccino, latte £1.95–2.50. Teas £1.50–£2 include Ethical Tea Partnership.

Children welcome, high chairs. Outside seating, dogs welcome, dog bowl, hoop to attach lead while you're at the counter. Wifi. MC, Visa.

Zest to Go

Omnivorous salad bar & juice bar

97 Market Street, St Andrews KY16 9NX
Tel: 01334–208 007
Open: Mon–Sat 08.30–17.30, Sun 11.00–17.00, can close earlier if busy, or later in summer

This branch is a salad bar with lots of vegan, healthy, low fat options and juices. It's mainly take–away but you can eat in. Salad bar small £2.95, regular £3.95, large £4.95, point to what you want from around 15 dishes (20 in summer). It's almost all vegetarian and plenty vegan such as quinoa, mung beans, chickpeas, roast veg.

Drinks are as at Zest but more juices and fewer smoothies.

Children welcome, no high chairs here. Outside seating, dogs welcome, dog bowl. Wifi. MC, Visa.

Also in St Andrews, **The Vine Leaf** at 131 South Street, open Tue–Sat from 18.00, has separate vegetarian menus, though almost everything contains egg or dairy. 2 courses £26.50. If they veganize some dishes, we'll put them in the next edition!
www.vineleafstandrews.co.uk

St Andrews Health Foods

Health and wholefood shop

123 Market Street, St Andrews, Fife KY16 9PE
Tel: 01334-478 887
Open: Mon–Sat 9.00–17.00, Sun closed
www.healthfoodstandrews.co.uk

In the main street, near the bus station. Lots of Fairtrade. Soya, oat, almond and rice milk. Local organic bread.
Fridge with vegan Bute Island Scheese, tofu sausages, hummus.
No freezer, but they can order in frozen food if you pick up the same day.
Vegan chocolate by Plamil, Montezuma. Bodycare includes Avalon, Faith in Nature, Weleda, Eco, Urtekram, Natracare.

Supplements by Solgar, Quest, Nature's Aid, Nature's Plus, Biocare, Higher Nature, Bio-Health, Lifeplan, Power Health, Viridian, sports nutrition. Weleda and Nelsons homeopathy, Bach and Jan de Vries flower remedies, A. Vogel tinctures. Essential oils.
Cleaning By Ecover, BioD. MC, Visa.

Holland & Barrett, Fife

Health food shops

Unit 31, Kingsgate Shopping Centre
Dunfermline., Fife KY12 7QU
Tel: 01383–624 915
Open: Mon–Sat 9.00–17.30,
Sun 12.00–16.00

22 Lyon Way, **Glenrothes**, Fife KY7 5NN
Tel: 01592–769 542
Open: Mon–Sat 9.00–17.00,
Sun 11.00–17.00

132 High Street, **Kirkcaldy**, Fife KY1 1NQ
Tel: 01592–205 349
Open: Mon–Sat 9.00–17.30,
Sun 11.00–17.00

104 Market Street, **St Andrews**, Fife KY16 9PB
Tel: 01334–473 148
Open: Mon–Sat 9.00–17.30,
Sun 11.30–16.30
www.hollandandbarrett.com

Fife Veg

Local group

Chris Childe, Cupar
chris@childe.co.uk
Facebook: Fife Veg

Open group on Facebook, they arrange social meals.

Morayshire

The Elms B&B

Vegetarian bed & breakfast

54 Fife Street, Dufftown AB55 4AP
Tel: 01340–820 471
Open: all year
Train: Keith, 20 minutes taxi, or bus
Huntly 40 minutes by taxi
www.theelmsdufftown.com

Victorian house owned by a Scottish–Canadian couple who are marine biologists, animal and whisky lovers, and expert on local attractions and visiting local distilleries.

Two doubles, one twin room, £26 per person, single occupancy £40, under-12 free in parents' room. Cot available with notice. Full cooked or continental vegetarian breakfast, or packed lunch if prefered. Vegans no problem with notice. Rooms have tv, tea/coffee making, clock radio, bathrobe (if more than one night), hairdryer, electric blanket in winter, free wifi. Iron available.

Off street parking. Secure parking for motorcycles and bicyles in locked garages. Extremely friendly resident cat. Guest fridge and ice. Welcoming whisky if you book online. Cash or travellers cheques only.

Fournet Guest House

Omnivorous B&B, vegetarian owners

16–20 Balvenie Street, Dufftown, Banffshire AB55 4AB
Tel: 01340–821428
Train: Huntly or Keith, 20 mins taxi or bus
www.fournethouse.co.uk

About 40 or 50 minutes' drive from Findhorn, the whole place is geared towards well-being and has a warm, creative and encouraging feel.

1 twin ensuite , 1 kingsize double with ensuite whirlpool bath, 1 four poster double , 1 single/small double. £30–41 per person. £10 for use of whirlpool which eats electricity. Vegetarian or vegan cooked breakfast. Well behaved children welcome, reduced rate if sharing with parents. No dogs. Rooms have tv or radio, tea/coffee making, soya milk available.

Guest living room with peat and log fire, tv, dvd, music, video, games, small library. Wellbeing and therapy garden. Norwegian therapy cats to stroke. Drying room. Laundry facilities available for small charge. Secure parking for bikes.

Noah's Ark Bistro

Omnivorous licensed bistro

18 Balvenie Street, Dufftown, Banffshire AB55 4AB
Tel: 01340–821 428
Open: 12.00 till the last person leaves at night
www.fournethouse.co.uk/bistro.html

Renovated in 2010, wholefood based cooking with plenty for vegetarians and vegans. Home-made bread. Some home-grown veg. The menu is ever-changing, light meals around £4.50–7.50, for example home-made soup, grilled veggie baguette, chickpea burger with salad or chips. Main courses £11.95 such as curry, veggie haggis. Desserts such as crumbles or rice pudding can be vegan.

Vegan wines from £13.50 bottle. Scottish ales. Smoothies.

Well behaved children of all ages welcome. High chair. No pets except guide dogs. Advance booking advised. Cash only, cashpoint nearby.

Dufftown is a little town in the hills with lovely walks, a good golf course and a scenic small railway to Keith and back. Tourist info:
www.dufftown.co.uk

Findhorn

The Findhorn Foundation is a spiritual community, eco-village and international centre for holistic education. It has a cafe, shop, events hall, retreat, bed and breakfasts and caravan park.

Bed and breakfast accommodation is available in many of the eco-houses that make up the community and they all have different room types and rates. For a full list, contact the Findhorn Foundation visitor centre: 01309-690 311 (9am-5pm) or visit the website: www.findhorn.org/visit/b-and-b/

The Blue Angel Cafe

Omnivorous organic cafe

At the entrance to the Universal Hall in Findhorn eco-village, **Forres** IV36 3TZ
Tel: 01309-691 900
Open: summer 9.00-17.00, winter 9-16.00
www.phoenixshop.co.uk/cafe

Mostly organic cafe in the Findhorn Foundation. Also an evening cafe/bar for events in the adjacent hall, when they are licensed.
The menu is both vegetarian and fish and very centred on cheese. Everything costs £3-4. Options include organic baked potato with beans or vegetable chilli, sandwiches and paninis. Soup with wholemeal roll, rice cakes or oatcakes, is usually vegan and gluten-free. Pizza can be made without cheese. Soya milk available.
Children welcome, high chairs. Outside seating, where you can smoke and bring a dog. Local art on the walls. Crockery from the nearby pottery. Cash only, but there's a cashpoint at the shop a few yards away.

Phoenix Community Store

Health food shop

The Park, Findhorn Bay, Forres IV36 3TZ
Tel: 01309-690 110
Open: Mon-Fri 10.00-18.00 (Wed from 11.00), Sun 11.00-17.00
www.phoenixshop.co.uk
Facebook: Phoenix Community Store

Community-owned wholefood supermarket at the entrance to Findhorn eco-village. Specialises in local, organic, Fairtrade and artisan foods. Stocks a wide range of organic fruit and vegetables, organic bread from a local baker, packaged, tinned and dry foods, teas, juices, beer and wine. Lots of chocolate. Large fridge and freezer with all the usual brands of meat and cheese substitutes, ready meals and tofu. Bodycare, re-usable nappies, cleaning products, supplements, remedies and aromatherapy oils.
They often run special promotions. Cashpoint just outside.

The Bakehouse Cafe

Omnivorous organic cafe

91–92 Findhorn, **Forres**, IV36 3YG
Tel: 01309–691 826
Open: Every day 10.00–16.00 (longer in summer, sometimes themed evenings)
www.bakehousecafe.co.uk

The Bakehouse cafe is in the village itself, rather than the Findhorn community. The menu is more meat-based than the Blue Angel cafe, though they have some veggie options such as veggieburger and potato wedges. Vegan options are very limited. They're big on local, ethical, Fairtrade, organic, slow food.
Full Scottish cooked breakfast with vegetarian bacon and sausage £7.95. Filled rolls £2.50 such as vegi bacon or sausage, extra fillings 75p.
Soup with bread £3.50. Paté and oatcakes with chutney and salad garnish £4.50. Salads £4.95–7.95. Filled baked potato £3.50, extra fillings £1 include baked beans or roast vegetables. Veggieburger £6.50 with wedges and salad garnish. Wedges £2.50.
Coffee £1.25–1.50, large £3.50, top ups 25p–50p. Pots of tea £1.50. Juices £1.50–£2. They have soya milk. Organic wines and beers when open in the evenings.
Children welcome, high chairs. Outside seating, dogs welcome there. MC, Visa.

For eating out in the evening in Forres, around the High Street you can find Italian, Indian and Thai restaurants.

Natural Balance Health Store

Health food shop

142 High Street, **Forres** IV36 1NP
Tel: 01309–694 824
Open: Mon–Sat 9.00–17.00
www.forresweb.net/forres–shops/
Natural Balance Health Store
Facebook: Natural Balance Health Store
www.backinbalance.co.uk

A small but well–stocked shop with a daily delivery of organic bread from the Findhorn Bakery.
They have a fridge with tofu, soya cream cheese and Bute Island vegan cheeses.
Flapjacks, raw chocolate, Nakd bars, Plamil and Olive Tree locally–produced chocolates.
Weleda, Jason, and Natracare bodycare. Supplements by Vogel, Higher Nature, Solgar and Meridian. Essential oils from local company Aromantic. Ecover and Suma cleaning products.
Resident osteopath, massage therapist, aromatherapist and reflexologist.
Local crafts, gifts, hand–made soaps and incense. Back care accessories, books and jewellery. MC, Visa, minimum spend £10.

Perth is a gateway to the Highlands and an excellent base for touring. By car it's half an hour from Dundee, less than an hour from Edinburgh, and just over an hour from Glasgow.

www.perthcity.co.uk
www.perthshire.co.uk
www.perthshire-scotland.co.uk
web.undiscoveredscotland.com/perth/perth
www.scone-palace.co.uk
www.pitlochry.org

Perth & Kinross

Lendrick Lodge

Vegetarian holistic retreat and spiritual centre

Brig O'Turk, A821, **Callander** FK17 8HR
Tel: 01877–376 263
Open: for retreats and courses all year
Office Mon–Fri 9.00–17.00
Train: Stirling then bus 59 to Callander then taxi £10 from Dreadnought Hotel or call 01877–330496
www.lendricklodge.com
Facebook: Lendrick Lodge

Since the mid eighties, centre for yoga, Reiki, shamanism, personal growth, detox retreats with meditation, massage and qi gong. For example detox weekend retreat £210 plus £100 for accommodation and meals. See website for all courses. Personal retreats £50 per day for accommodation and meals, or £32 accommodation and breakfast. Lunch or dinner £9. All meals are vegetarian and often vegan, and they can do special diets.

Standard rooms sleep 3–4. Add £6 per person for twin/double, £12 for single, £6 for ensuite.

Some courses are suitable for teenagers or children. No pets.

Rosebank House

Omnivorous guest house

Main Street, **Strathyre**, Loch Lomond & Trossachs National Park, Callander FK18 8NA (8 miles north of Callander)
Tel: 01877–384 208
Open: all year
Train: Stirling 23 miles, Dunblane 15 miles, then bus or they can collect
www.rosebankhouse.co.uk
enquiries@www.rosebankhouse.co.uk

Victorian house in a bonnie village, well situated for walkers, golfers, cyclists and bird watchers. Nearby are Stirling Castle, Loch Lomond, Glencoe and distilleries. They get a lot of vegetarians and have a separate breakfast menu for us with vegan haggis (lentils, carrots, turnips, onion and mushroom) and Lincolnshire sausages (tofu and soya).

Doubles and twins ensuite or with private bathroom £32 per person, single occupancy £42 or Jul–Aug £64. 10% off for 3+ nights except Aug. Nov–Mar 3 nights for the price of two.

Children welcome, under 12 half price, U–5 free. Cot. Dogs welcome.

Rooms have tv/dvd and tea/coffee making. Free wifi. Conservatory. Summer house. Large garden with views. Guest lounge with tv, dvd, Xbox, board games. Maps and books and one of the owners is a keen walker. Drying room. MC, Visa.

Lendrick Lodge vegetarian retreat centre, Callander

Ardfern Guest House

Omnivorous guest house

15 Pitcullen Crescent, Perth PH2 7HT
(on A94 Perth/Coupar Angus/Forfar Road,
walking distance from the centre)
Tel: 01738-637 031
Open: all year
www.ardfernguesthouse.co.uk

Double and family (double and single)
ensuite, twin with private bathroom,
£25-30 per person, or single occupancy
£40-45, reductions for long stays and
winter. Children half price, up to 2 years
free. High chair and cot.
Rooms have tv, free wifi.
Full Scottish cooked vegetarian
breakfast including Linda McCartney
sausages. No dogs, they have one. Off
street car parking. Guest lounge with
open fire. Scottish Tourist Board 4 stars.

Rowanlea Guest House

Omnivorous guest house

87 Glasgow Road, Perth PH2 0PQ
(15 mins walk from tourist info centre)
Tel: 01738-621 922
Open: all year except Xmas-New Year
www.rowanlea-guesthouse.co.uk

All rooms ensuite, one twin, two
doubles, £32-35 per person, one single
£38-45. Especially popular with
couples, not so suitable for children.
They get lots of vegetarians here.
Cooked vegetarian breakfast, vegans
with notice, plus many kinds of fresh
fruit.
Rooms have tv, hairdryer, hospitality
tray, wifi, ironing facilites. One ground
floor room. Sunny lounge. Off street car
parking. MC, Visa.

Cocoa Mountain,Aucherarder

Vegetarian chocolate cafe and shop

154 High Street, Auchterarder,
Perthshire PH3 1AD
Tel: 01764-663 105
Open: Mon–Fri 8.30–19.00, Sat 8.30–17.00,
Sun 11.00–16.00; closed Dec 25-6, Jan 1-2
www.cocoamountain.co.uk

Sister to their original shop in Durness (see Highlands). All the chocolates and truffles are gluten-free and some are vegan, including Turkish Delight, and even a vegan chocolate hamper for £70. Also vegan hot chocolate, mocha, organic coffee, cappuccino, latte, teas, organic cold drinks. They have soya milk. Also croissants, scones, cake, biscuits, many gluten-free but none vegan. Also online store.

Jan de Vries Health & Diet Centre

Health food shop

125 High Street, Auchterarder PH3 1AA
Tel: 01764-660 246
Open: Mon–Sat 9.30–17.30
www.jandevrieshealth.co.uk

The latest store in the chain opened October 2011. Quite a big shop with all the usual wholefoods. No fridge or freezer. Vegan chocolate by Moo Free, Booja Booja, Ma Baker bars, Nakd.
Bodycare by Weleda, Pukka, Barefoot SOS, Faith in Nature, Avalon Organics, Organic Surge, Green People, Dead Sea Magik, Natracare, Weleda Baby, Green Baby.
Supplements by Solgar, Quest, Lamberts, Optima, Lifeplan, Pukka, Nature's Aid. Weleda homeopathy, New Era tissue salts, a few essential oils. Consultation room, with Jan de Vries visiting occasionally and they are lining up practitioners.

Cleaning by Ecover, Method. Jan de Vries books. Candles, incense. Christmas gift baskets. MC, Visa.

Nature's Corner

Health food shop

2a Cross Street, Callander FK17 8EA
(corner of Main Street)
Tel: 01877-330 200
Open: Mon–Sat 9.30–17.30, Sun Apr–Dec 12.00–17.00; may be longer hours in summer and shorter in winter
www.incallander.co.uk/naturecorner.htm
www.natures-corner.com (online shop)

Lots of gluten-free products. A. Vogel (Bioforce) specialist shop with staff trained to advise on products. One of the owners is vegetarian. A lot of tourists call in here all year round.
Fridge and freezer with Wicken Fen, Realeat, Redwood, Bute Island Scheese, tofu, frozen tempeh, Swedish Glace.
Bodycare by Nature's Response, Weleda, Faith in Nature, Mason's Dog Oil (great for rheumatism, not for dogs). Supplements by Solgar, Nature's Aid, A Vogel, Lifeplan, Power Health. Some Weleda, New Era and Nelsons homeopathy and a few essential oils.
Ecover, Earth Friendly, BioD, Ecoegg, Attitude cleaning. Free magazines. If you're after anything special, they can get it within a week, even vegetarian dog food. MC, Visa.

There's a good baker nearby. Callander is on the main A84 road from Stirling to the Highlands and to Oban, Fort William and the Western Islands. This shop is on the junction with the A81 from Glasgow. The town has lots of accommodation though the Brook Linn vegetarian B&B has now closed.

Delicious

Omnivorous sandwich bar and coffee shop

46 South Methven Street, Perth PH1 5NX
Tel: 01738-451 617
Open: Mon-Sat 9.30-16.30, Sun closed
www.facebook.com/pages/Delicious/15239
6691452014

Very friendly, quirky little cafe. They have local vegetarians coming here every day.
Salad box £3.20, point to what you want. Sandwiches to order from £2.70, vegans could have peanut butter. Always a vegetarian soup, sometimes vegan, £2.10. Filled baked potatoes from £3.95.
Homemade cakes and tray bakes £1.20-1.60, none vegan.
Pot of tea or herb tea £1.50. Coffee £1.80, cappuccino and latte £2.20. No soya milk. Juices and soft drinks from £1.30.
Children welcome, smaller portions, high chair, kids' books. One bench outside, dogs welcome. Cash only.

Glassrooms at Perth Concert Hall

Omnivorous cafe-bar

Perth Concert Hall, Mill Street, Perth PH1 5HZ
Tel: 01738-477 724
Open: Mon-Sat 10.00-16.30; show evenings till performance ends which can be as late as 00.30; sometimes open Sun
www.horsecross.co.uk/
food-and-drink/glassrooms

Vegetarian, dairy-free and gluten-free dishes are marked. Soup with bread £3.25. Hummus with salad and pitta or oatcakes £3.50. Hummus salad sandwich £3.85-4.25. Veggieburger with chips and salad £6.75. Pasta with courgette, mushroom and shallot in tomato and basil sauce £5.45, half portion £3.65. No vegan cakes.
Soft drinks around £1.50-£2. Pot of tea £1.60-1.85. Coffee, latte, cappuccino, mocha, hot choc £1.65-2.60. No soya milk. Fully licensed, wine £3.55 medium glass, £5 large, £14.75 bottle.
Very family friendly, high chairs, breast-feeding friendly, lots of children's events. Disabled access. MC, Visa.

Pizza Express, Perth

Omnivorous Italian restaurant

16 South Methven Street, Perth PH1 5PE
Tel: 01738–628 733
Open: Sun–Thu 11.30–22.00, Fri–Sat 23.00
www.pizzaexpress.com

For menu see Glasgow. Disabled access. Children welcome, baby changing.

Sante

Omnivorous wine bar & restaurant

10 St. John's Place, Perth PH1 5SU
Tel: 01738–449 710
Food: Sun–Thu 10.00–22.00, Fri–Sat 23.00
Bar open later, Thu till 23.30, Fri–Sat 24.00
www.sante–winebar.co.uk
Facebook: Santé Winebar & Restaurant

The main menu is meaty, but there is a tapas menu £3.50–3.90 a portion, with salads, crostini and dips, patatas bravas etc. Chips £2.50. 12.00–19.30 you can get three tapas and bread £9.90, with a small glass of wine £12.90. House wines £3 small glass, £14.95 bottle. MC, Visa, Amex.

Tabla Indian Restaurant

Omnivorous Indian restaurant

173 South Street, Perth PH2 8NY (at King St)
Tel: 01738–444 630
Mobile: 07855 566649
Open: Mon–Sat 12.00–14.30, 17.00–22.30,
Sun 15.00–22.30
www.tablarestaurant.co.uk

The owners are south Indian vegetarians. Lunch £6.95 is pakora or bhajia, then dal or jalfrezi veg with rice or nan. Evening curries £6.95, rice £1.95–2.95, dosas £4.95. Starters and mains are vegan, but no vegan desserts. Takeaways cheaper.
Children very welcome, high chairs. Fully licensed with a bar. House wine £3.45 small glass, £12.95 bottle. MC, Visa.

Highland Health Store

Health food shop

7 and 16 St Johns Street, Perth PH1 5SP
Wholefoods at 7: 01738–455038
Remedies at 16: 01738–628102
Open: Mon–Fri 8.45–17.15, Sat 8.45–17.00
www.perthcitydirectory.co.uk/healthstore

Vegan heaven, the best place in Perth to grab lunch, with stacks of vegan savouries. They can heat up food in a microwave for eating outside on a bench in the pedestrianised street. There are two shops facing each other, one called Wholefoods, one called Remedies.

Wholefoods at number 7 sells all the usual dry wholefoods, teas, Japanese foods, nuts, seeds, dried fruit, gluten-free foods. Wholemeal and spelt bread. Best of all is the very impressive take-away section that is a delight for vegan self-caterers and walkers. They have Forest Foods' burritos, smoked tofu calzone, chickpea and spinach calzone, mushroom and sage rolls; also Saker Bakery rolls, pasties, vegan cakes, flapjacks. Vegan chocolate by Organica, Montezuma, Plamil, Moo Free, Dairy Free buttons, Fabulous Fudge Factory vegan fudge. Ma Baker giant bars. Nakd range.

Fridge and freezer with Redwood Cheatin' range, Dragonfly, Bute Island Sheese, Taifun tofu sausages, soya yogurts, Engine Shed tofu, Frys/Beanies, Swedish Glace ice-cream in four flavours, Mama Cucina vegan cheese-cake. Fresh or frozen vegan haggis.

Cleaning by Faith in Nature, Ecover and refills. Natracare.

Remedies at number 16 stocks lots of brands that are hard to find locally. Bodycare by Green People, Weleda, Jason, Faith in Nature, Tisserand, Le Petit Olivier (with argon oil), Organic Baby and Children, Earth Friendly Baby, Green Baby, Weleda Baby. At Christmas they do lots of gift boxes.

Supplements by A.Vogel, Solgar, Nature's Plus, Nature's Aid, Viridian and lots more. Sports nutrition. Weleda and some Nelson's homeopathy, Bach flower full range. Natural by Nature aromatherapy. Food intolerance screening bimonthly. A computer service can check the compatibility of supplements against prescribed medicines.

Magnetic bracelets and bangles. MC, Visa.

Holland & Barrett, Perth

Health food shops

187 High Street, Perth PH1 5UN
Tel: 01738–628 115
Open: Mon–Sat 9.00–17.30, Sun 11–16.00

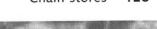

Stirlingshire

Tir na nOg
Holistic Centre

Holistic centre with vegetarian catering, vegetarian cafe and shop

Tir na nOg Holistic Centre, Balfunning, Balfron
Station, Stirlingshire G63 0NF
Tel: 01360–449 300
Cafe open: Tue–Sun 10.30–17.00,
Mon closed
Bus: Stirling to Glasgow route, twice daily
www.tirnanog.co.uk
Facebook: Tir na nOg Holistic Centre

Holistic centre in the grounds of a country estate on the edge of the Loch Lomond and Trossachs National Park, 40 minutes from Glasgow and 30 minutes from Stirling. It's right beside the West Highland Way walking route so there are lots of bed and breakfasts nearby. Therapies, New Age and personal growth workshops. Cafe opening hours currently under review: call ahead or check website before coming.

Cafe uses local and organic where possible, with light meals prepared to order. Vegan soup of the day £3.50 with scone, bread or oatcakes. Wraps £3.50, sandwiches £4, toasted panini £4.50. Soup and wrap, pitta, sandwich or panini £6–6.50. Salads £4.50 with bread, scone or oatcakes. There are always vegan options such as hummus. Fruit scones, cakes, chocolate brownies, flapjacks £1.25–2.75. Afternoon tea with sandwiches, cakes, scones and hot drink £10, children £5. Teas £1.70. Fairtrade coffee, latte, cappuccino, hot choc, mocha £1.50–2.25. They usually have soya milk.

Very child friendly, high chairs, baby changing, toys. Dogs welcome. Some outside seating. MC, Visa.

Therapies around £30–50 a session include many kinds of massage, reflexology, Reiki, NLP, EFT, counselling and psychotherapy, medical herbalism.

Shop sells crystals, books, jewellery, music, candles, herbs, oils, and unusual gifts.

They have contact details for local accommodation and most of them can accommodate vegetarians. The centre can be hired for family and business events and parties.

Bistro @the Campus

Omnivorous cafe

Raploch Community Campus Bistro, Forth
Valley College, Drip Road, Stirling FK8 1RD
Tel: 01786-272 317
College: 01786-27 23 00
Open: Mon-Fri 10.00-16.00, Sat-Sun closed
www.forthvalley.ac.uk/campus/
raploch_community_campus

Forth Valley college restaurant is open
to the public and caters quite well for
veggies and also has some vegan and
gluten-free dishes.

Lite bites from £2.95, main courses
from £3.50, such as nachos, salad,
risotto, savoury vegetable tartlet.
Desserts are not vegan.

Fairtrade coffee from 90p, latte or
cappuccino £1.70, tea and herb teas
from 70p. They sometimes have soya
milk on request.

Children welcome, high chairs, baby
changing. No dogs. MC, Visa.

You can also visit the salon next door
for a hair cut, waxing, manicure or
Indian head massage by trainees, book
on 01786-272 315.

Stirling Health Food Store

Wholefood and health food shop

29 Dumbarton Road, Stirling FK8 2LQ
Tel: 01786-464 903
Open: Mon-Sat 9.00-17.30, bank holidays
10.00-16.00, closed Sun and Xmas
www.stirlinghealthfoodstore.co.uk

All the usual wholefoods, dairy- and
gluten-free, and health foods like
beetroot and acai juice, goji berries, and
a hundred kinds of tea.

Fridge with Bute Island Sheese, Engine
Shed tofu and smoked tofu, tempeh,
sometimes veggie sausages but they
sell fast. No freezer. Organica vegan
chocolate.

Bodycare by Weleda, Jason, Faith in
Nature, Thursday Plantation, Toms,
Natracare, Mooncup, Green People and
Earth Friendly Baby and Children.

Supplements by Solgar, Nature's Aid.
Quest, Viridian, Lifeplan, A. Vogel.
Weleda and New Era homeopathy.
Vogel, Bach and Ainsworth flower
remedies and Bioforce range for pets.
Full range of Natural by Nature essential
oils. Homeopath round the corner.

Cleaning by BioD, Ecover, Faith in
Nature Clear Spring and can order
others.

Pet food including vegetarian organic
Yarrah. Home brewing supplies. They
can order in anything else you need and
bulk wholefoods up to 25kg: email or
phone to request. MC, Visa.

Stirling Raw Food Group

Social group

www.meetup.com/
Stirling-Raw-Food-Meetup-Group

Come and socialise with other people
who are interested in raw and living
foods. Regular potlucks to share raw
vegan food, recipes and conversation.

Stirling tourist info:
www.visitstirling.org

The Real Food Cafe

Omnivorous cafe

Main Street, Tyndrum, Loch Lomond and The
Trossachs National Park FK20 8RY
Tel: 01838-400 235
Open: summer: Mon–Fri 11.30–21.00,
Sat 9.00–21.00, Sun 10.00–21.00;
Oct: Mon, Thu 12.00–20.00, Fri 12.00–21.30,
Sat–Sun 12.00–21.00, Tue–Wed closed;
Jan–Mar: Fri–Sun 12.00–20.00
www.therealfoodcafe.com
www.facebook.com/pages/
The–Real–Food–Cafe/177987785553736

Roadside cafe with a few vegetarian and vegan options and
organic drinks. Vegetable soup
with crusty bread £4.20. Veg and
chickpea curry and chips £6.95.
Mushroom tempura £3.95. Large
onion rings £2.95. Salads £3.45 to
£8.25 for roast veg and pine kernel
salad. Rosti £4.50.

Holland & Barrett, Stirling

Health food shops

45 High Street, **Falkirk**, Stirlingshire FK1 1ES
Tel: 01324-633 397
Open: Mon–Sat 9.00–17.30, Sun 11–16.00

Thistle Centre, **Stirling** FK8 2ED
Tel: 01786-465 350
Open: Mon–Fri 9.00–17.30, Thu 20.00, Sat
9.00–18.00, Sun 11.00–17.00

Stirlingshire SCOTLAND

To visit the Highlands really means getting away from it all. The area contains the best scenery in Britain, remote white-washed crofts and herds of shaggy orange cattle. The Gaelic language is widely-spoken here, though everybody speaks English too.

Sutherland and **Wester Ross** are remote, stunning and wind-swept, with few towns and mostly single track roads, but plenty of wildlife spotting and mountai climbing opportunities. **Ullapool** is a tiny, beautiful town with a thriving arts scene, two vegetarian bed and breakfasts and mountains that slope right down to the harbour.

Fort William is set amidst some of the most beautiful scenery in Scotland and is just around the corner from Ben Nevis, the highest mountain in Britain. The town relies on tourists and is ideal for a quiet walking holiday, or a more active skiing, rock climbing, canoeing or cycling fix. Also nearby is the Ben Nevis Distillery, where visitors can take a tour.

Kingussie is an excellent centre for touring the Central Highlands. It's within easy reach of the **Aviemore** ski slopes and the western half of the **Cairngorms**, a National Park with some very remote forests filled with deer and red squirrels. The area offers lots of outdoor activities such as hill walking, mountaineering, natural history tours, skiing and snowboarding. There's also a Folk Museum, Wildlife Park and a Whisky Trail. **Loch Ness** is an hour's drive.

If you want city culture both traditional and modern, head for **Inverness**, which is well-linked by road, air and rail.

There's little to see at the famous **John o'Groats** besides a ferry terminal to Orkney, but people travel there just to say they've stood at the northeastern-most point in mainland Britain. The northernmost point is actually the wind-blasted **Dunnet Head,** which has a small nature reserve, car park and hotel.

Highland Wholefoods in Inverness is the perfect place to stock up on supplies, and they also supply many remote shops.

Highlands

Nevis View

Omnivorous B&B (vegetarian owned)

14 Farrow Drive, **Corpach, Fort William**,
Inverness-shire PH33 7JW (4 miles from town
centre, 3 buses until 5pm, then hourly)
Train: Corpach (Glasgow to Mallaig line)
Tel: 01397-772 447
Mobile: 07570 133 425
Open: all year, but check for Xmas
www.nevisviewfortwilliam.co.uk
enquiries@nevisviewfortwilliam.co.uk

3 rooms, one with double, one single,
plus Easter to end Aug one
double/single, from £22.50 per person,
from £30 single occupancy. Children 4–
13 £12.50 sharing with 2 adults, or full
price in own room. Family room with
double and single, good for family of 4
using adjacent single at under-14 rate.
Rooms have tv, clock radio, hospitality
tray. Cooked vegetarian or vegan
breakfast available, just be sure to tell
them when booking.
Packed lunch £5; 2 or 3 course evening
meal £12.50-£15 with 24 hours notice.
Well behaved dogs welcome with own
bedding. Drying room. Bike and ski
storage. Hairdryer available. Wifi.

Rhu Mhor Guest House

Omni guest house, veggie owners

Alma Road, **Fort William**, Inverness-shire
PH33 6BP
Tel: 01397-702 213
Train: Fort William, 10 mins walk
Open: Easter–October
www.rhumhor.co.uk
ian.macpherson12@btinternet.com

Set in an acre of wild tree-shrouded
garden, overlooking Loch Linnhe and
the hills of Loch Eil. Veggie kilt-wearing
proprietor!
7 rooms, 4 ensuite. Standard double or
twin £21-25 per person. Double or twin

ensuite £29-33. Children 4–12 years
sharing with 2 adults £14-17 in family
or triple, charged as adults if in their
own room. Under 3 no charge. Three
adults sharing 10% discount. Single
occupancy £29-59 according to room
and season.
Light or full cooked breakfast, can cater
for vegans. Rooms have washbasins,
tea and coffee making. Cot. Tv lounge
and separate sitting room. MC, Visa.

Sonnhalde

Omnivorous guest house

East Terrace, **Kingussie**, Highlands PH21 1JS
Tel: 01540-661 266
Train Station: Kingussie 1/2 mile, then
owners can collect
Open: all year
www.sonnhalde.co.uk
sonn.gh@btopenworld.com

Victorian villa with an open outlook
across the Spey Valley to the Cairngorm
mountains. Seven rooms: 2 doubles
ensuite £30 per person; 3 twins ensuite
or with private bathroom £27-30; large
ensuite family room, 4 single beds, £30;
double plus adult bunk beds with
shared bathroom, £26 each. Children
under 16 half price.
Hearty vegetarian or vegan breakfast
includes muesli or porridge, buckwheat
crepes with tomatoes and mushrooms.
Tea and coffee making in rooms, tv by
request. Lounge with tv.

Cuildorag House

Veggie bed and breakfast with three rooms amidst some of Britain's most magnificent landscapes. The double and family room are £27.50 per person per night, single occupancy £40, and the double ensuite is £32.50 per person, single occupancy £50. Families from £66. For one night's stay add 10%, subject to availability. Children under 2 stay for free.

Breakfast is cereal or porridge followed by veggie sausages, potato scone, baked beans, mushrooms and tomatoes, Fairtrade tea or coffee. Vegan margarine and soya milk are always available and sometimes soya yogurt. A three course dinner is offered by arrangement for £20, such as home-made soup with chilli scones or hummus with garlic toasts followed by stuffed pancakes, winter vegetable crumble or sesame and lemon stir-fry and finish with pavlova with fresh fruit. Organic produce is mainly used, sometimes from the garden. There are veggie options at restaurants in nearby Fort William.

Fort William is a popular tourist centre and is close to the ski fields of Ben Nevis (Britain's highest mountain) and Glencoe. Skiing, snowboarding, hiking, climbing and bike riding are top activities in the area and you'll find plenty of shops where you can buy or hire equipment. There are walks for all levels, from strolls along Glen Nevis through the gorge to Steall Meadows, to the strenuous hike up Ben Nevis. Or you could embark on an eighty mile bike ride along the Great Glen Cycle Route which links Fort William and Inverness.

The Isles of Skye or Mull make great day trips.

All three rooms have a television and tea and coffee making facilities. Lounge with wood-burning stove, books and music. The garden attracts wildlife including red squirrels, deer and badgers.

Vegetarian bed and breakfast

Onich
near Fort William
West Highlands PH3 6SD
Scotland

Tel: 01855-821 529

www.cuildoraghouse.com
enquiries@cuildoraghouse.com

Train Station: Fort William, 10 miles, then a bus

Open: Mar–Nov

Directions: from the south, it is half a mile past Onich village store. Take the left turn signposted for Ardrhu / Cuilcheanna / Cuildorag House, look for their sign. From the north, just over a mile past the Corran Ferry. Come through the Onich sign and look for the next turning on the right.

Parking: available

There is a cot and the proprietor may even babysit for you

No dogs in the house (but ok to sleep in your car)

Smoking in the garden only

5% discount on stays of two nights or more to members of the Vegetarian Society, the Vegan Society, Viva! and people presenting this book

131

Lazy Duck Hostel

Self-catering hostel, cottage, camping and eco hut

Badanfhuarain, **Nethy Bridge**, Inverness-shire PH25 3ED
Train: Aviemore, then £24 taxi ride, or bus
Open: all year, camping Easter to end Oct
Tel: 01479-821 642
www.lazyduck.co.uk
Mobile calendar:
lazyduck.co.uk/mobile.html
lazyduckhostel@gmail.com

The Lazy Duck in the Cairngorms National Park is one of Scotland's smallest hostels sleeping only eight people in an open plan sleeping gallery £15 per person. Private use by arrangement. Well equipped kitchen, with home baked bread on request. No smoking.

Also woodman's hut for two £60 per night, or £150 for two nights weekend, can also take a baby under 1.

Cottage for 5 with double, twin and single plus cot. Pets by arrangement in the cottage only. From under £20 per person per night, see website for full details.

Advance groceries delivery service. Village shop one mile. Linen provided, bring own towels. Safe cycle storage. Washing machine and dryer by arrangement. Organic veg and salads grown on site. Sauna.

Corry Lodge

Vegetarian bed & breakfast

Garve Road, Lochbroom, **Ullapool,** Wester Ross IV26 2TB
Tel: 01854-612 777
Train: Inverness, 60 miles
Open: all year
www.corrylodge-ullapool.co.uk
Email: corrygarve@btinternet.com

Self-contained log cabin in one and a half acres of garden surrounded by woodlands, overlooking the loch and hills. One twin and one double bedroom, £27 per person. An extra bed can be put in the twin for £65 total per night. Children and animals welcome.

Lounge/dining room, bathroom, kitchenette, microwave and fridge, although no cooker. However the vegetarian owners, who cook with seasonal organic ingredients, will bring cooked breakfast over to you. Vegans no problem.

Nearby are nature walks, the beach and sailing. The picturesque port town is a walk away and has a museum, theatre, pubs with live music and numerous restaurants serving vegetarian food.

The cabin has all amenities including an iron and hairdryer. Televisions in the bedrooms. High chairs, toy box and cot. Be careful not to trip over one of the hens that run free in the garden.

Suilven

Vegetarian bed & breakfast

Rhue, **Ullapool**, Ross-shire IV26 2TJ
Tel: 01854-612 955
www.bvegb.co.uk
www.highlandpeaks.co.uk
info@bvegb.co.uk

This eco-home uses passive solar energy and a ground-sourced heat pump gives underfloor heating and hot water, supplemented by a solar panel and wood-burning stove in winter.

One double ensuite, one twin, call for prices.

Living room and sun room with views over the sea loch and mountains. Friendly cats.

The owner is a qualified mountain leader who offers guided walking and navigation courses.

Nearby restaurants include Indian and Chinese.

Little Hill of my Heart

Omnivorous bed & breakfast

Meall mo Chridhe, Cammusterach,
Applecross IV54 8LU
Tel: 01520-744 432
www.applecrossaccommodation.co.uk

3 double rooms ensuite or with private bathroom, £32.50–£45 per person. Single by arrangement. No children under 12 (no family room).

The vegetarian breakfasts are truly amazing and as a result many non-veggies choose them. Their vegan menu for example includes juice, cereals, fresh fruit salad, soya yogurt, croustade of mushrooms, brazil nut roast haggis, soya and chickpea sausages. All vegan cooked dishes are home-made. They even make their own granola, muesli and bread.

No dogs, they have one. Rooms have wifi. One room is downstairs. Cash or cheque only.

Nearby the Applecross Inn and The Walled Garden cater for veggies and vegans.

For more on the area see the links page on their website.

Sleeperzzz

Self-catering hostel

Rogart Station, Pittentrail, **Rogart**, Sutherland IV28 3XA
Tel: 01408-641 343
Text/mobile: 07833 641226
Open: beginning Mar – end Sep
Train: Rogart (on Inverness Wick/Thurso Far North line, 4 trains daily each way, one on Sunday)
www.sleeperzzz.com
kate@sleeperzzz.com

Budget hostel in a train in an unspoilt crofting village, ideal for families, back-packers, walkers and cyclists. 26 beds.

Two carriages each have 4 compart-ments, sleeping two in each, plus shared kitchen, dining room, living area, toilets and showers.

Another carriage has two self-contained sections, one with two beds, the other with two compartments sleeping two in each. Both sections have own kitchen, dining room, living area, toilet and shower.

A showman's wagon has one double bed and living area. Renovated Bedford SB bus has two beds and living area. These use cooking and toilet facilities in the adjacent carriages.

£15 per person, children under 12 £10, 10% discount for guests arriving by bicycle or rail. Free bicycle hire for guests. Bedding supplied, bring towels. No pets. Cash or cheque only. No smoking.

Spar shop 100m away which sells organic muesli. Great for hill walking or cycling, and sampling malt whiskies in the inn 100m away which does vege-tarian food though not vegan. See website for full details and pictures.

Mountain Cafe

Omnivorous cafe

111 Grampian Road, Aviemore PH22 1RH
Tel: 01479–812 473
Open winter: Sat–Mon 8.30–17.30, Tue–Fri
8.30–17.00; summer till 17.30 every night
www.mountaincafe-aviemore.co.uk
Facebook: Mountain Cafe Aviemore

Scottish cafe with a kiwi twist, a huge
Facebook following, and menus that
indicate the many items that are veggie,
vegan, dairy–free, gluten–free or
wheat–free. Go through the mountain
shop to get to the cafe upstairs. Views of
the Cairngorms.
Breakfast till 11.30 from £1.50 for toast
and spreads to £8.75 for a monster
veggie all day cooked breakfast with
filter coffee or tea. They even have
vegan muesli £5.95 with poached
plums, fresh fruit and berries. Red lentil
and chunky veggieburger £9 with
seasoned fries.
Lunch from 11.30 till they close. Soup
£3.75, with a wrap £6.95 such as
hummus falafel with couscous and
salad. Wrap on its own £5.20. Salad
£9.50 includes chickpeas, charred veg,
pine nuts and roasted sweet potato.
Filled baked potato £6.75. Fries £2.50.
They can also do you a packed lunch £6
for wrap, cake, crisps and a drink.
Stacks of cakes £2.80–£3 include a
vegan carrot, fruit and nut cake, berry
pine flapjack.
Coffee, latte, cappuccino £2.20–2.60,
they have soya milk. Tea £1.50. Juices
and cans £1.80–2.10. Wine £4.35 small
glass. Cairngorm Brewery local beers
£4.50.
Children's menu; high chairs. No dogs.
MC, Visa.

Fort William isn't the best place in the
world for vegetarians and watch out for
high prices. You can find Indian,
Chinese, Thai and Italian on the High
Street. Here are some possibilities
recommended to us by vegans who
have visited Fort William:
Mango Thai/Indian at 24 High Street.
Cafe 115 at 115 do nice coffees, meals
in the evening including vegetarian as a
matter of course.
Everest Indian at 141.
Highland Star Chinese at 155.

Ben Nevis Inn

Omnivorous pub & self–cater hostel

Claggan, Achintee PH33 6TE
Tel: 01397–701 227.
Open: Apr–Oct Mon–Sun 12.00–23.00,
late Oct–Apr Thu–Sun only, 12.00–23.00
Food served until 21.00
www.ben-nevis-inn.co.uk

At the start of the track up Ben Nevis,
caters veggie and vegan. Really nice
atmosphere say local veggies.
Spring rolls with salad leaves and sweet
chilli dip £5.75. Roasted vegetables in a
tomato sauce topped with a nut roast
crumble £8.95. Bowl of chips £2.50.
Half portions for children.
The hostel bunkhouse is a good place to
sleep just before climbing Ben Nevis,
and go afterwards for a pint and a good
rest. 24 beds in three sections, around
£15 per night. Bunks have duvet and all
bed linen, no sleeping bags allowed.
Showers. Large kitchen. Drying area. It's
very popular with walkers and moun-
taineers so advance booking is strongly
recommended. MC, Visa.

Julian Graves, Fort William

Health food shop

17-19 High St, Fort William PH33 6DH
Tel: 01397-705 482
Open: Mon-Sat 9.00-17.30, Sun closed

Lots of high energy nuts, dried fruits and snacks.

Also in Fort William we hear there are lots of wholefoods at **Morrisons**, open every day 8.00-21.00, Sun 9.00-18.00. Less in Tesco though they are opening a megastore at the end of 2012.

Tourist info:
www.visit-fortwilliam.co.uk

Inverness - Highlands **SCOTLAND**

Riverdale Centre Organic Cafe
Omnivorous organic cafe & shop

105–107 Church Street, Inverness IV1 1EY
Tel: 01463–250 589
Open: Mon–Sat 9.00–17.00, Sun closed
www.therapies–inverness.co.uk

The omnivorous cafe is the best place to eat in Inverness for veggies. Everything is home-made and they use local organic veg, and organic bread from Findhorn, with the option of oatcakes and gluten-free bread too.
Soup and a roll or savoury muffin £3.95 (note the muffins are not vegan but could be if it's a gluten-free one). Sandwich with salad £4.60–4.95, include hummus, roast red pepper hummus, patés. Soup and sandwich combo £6.20–6.60. Toasties £3–4.50. For something more substantial they are building a range of daily specials such as falafel or veggieburger £4.95.
Home-made cakes £2.20 and cookies £1.75–£2, always a gluten-free and vegan cake, usually sugar-free, such as carrot, apple, orange, pumpkin seed and raisin cake.
Coffees £1.95–2.50. Tea £1.75. They have soya milk. Organic vegetable juices, fruit smoothies and soft drinks.
Children welcome, no high chair but they have high stools. MC, Visa.
The small organic **shop** has breads, local organic veg and herbs, local organic salad bags from Easter till November, and many gluten-free and vegan products.
Therapies in the centre include acupuncture, Alexander technique, psychotherapy, hypnotherapy, herbal medicine, homeopathy, massage, osteopathy, physiotherapy, reflexology, Reiki, shiatsu, nutrition.

Pizza Express
Omnivorous restaurant

Unit B Eastgate Centre, Inverness IV2 3PP
(near the train station)
Tel: 01463–709 700
Open: Sun–Wed 11.30–22.00, Thu–Sat 22.30
www.pizzaexpress.com

For menu see Glasgow. Live jazz Thursday evening. Baby changing. Outside seating.

Most places in Inverness town centre cater for vegetarians. Some suggestions from locals:
Aspendos Turkish at 26 Queensgate IV1 1DJ.
George's Thai & South Indian at 19 Queensgate IV1 1DF.
Rendezvous Cafe at 14a Church Street IV1 1EA.
The Rajah Indian at 2 Post Office Ave IV1 1DN.
Riva Italian at 4–6 Ness Walk IV3 5NE.
Yum Cafe at 14a Margaret Street IV1 1LS (open till 6pm).

Highland Wholefoods

Vegetarian wholefood distributor

Highland Wholefoods Workers Cooperative,
Unit 6, 13 Harbour Road, Inverness IV1 1SY
(opposite Inverness College on the Longman
Industrial Estate, 10 mins walk from the main
bus and train stations)
Tel: 01463–712 393
Showroom: 01463–712 696
Fax: 01463–715 586
Open: Mon–Fri 9.00–17.00, Sat 10.00–16.00
www.highlandwholefoods.co.uk
www.facebook.com/HighlandWholefoods
sales@highlandwholefoods.co.uk

Organic, vegetarian, GM-free and
Fairtrade products. Bulk buy warehouse
at the back, retail showroom at the front
which is a regular wholefood shop. They
have supplied local communities in the
Highlands, Islands and north-east
Scotland since 1989, even the remotest
areas.

You can come in, browse and select
your own order. Or phone first then
phone, fax or email your order for
delivery or collection. There's a price list
on the website, click the Products tab on
the home page. If you're self-catering
and get your order in a week ahead,
they can deliver to your accommodation. No minimum order.

The shop has fresh bread. Fridge and
freezer with vegan cheeses, meat
substitutes, hummus, tofu, vegan ice-
cream by Swedish Glace. Japanese
products.

Vegan chocolate by Plamil, Moo Free,
Booja Booja, Divine, Organica,
Montezuma.

All their wine is vegan organic. Beer,
cider. Whisky on special order.

Bodycare by Faith in Nature, Weleda,
Green People, Kingfisher, Caurnie
soaps, Toms, Natracare. Maltex and
Bambino nappies, Hipp and Ella's
Kitchen baby food.

Cleaning by Ecover, BioD, Clearspring,
Fodasan, Earth Friendly and Faith in
Nature.

Some supplements and remedies. Aqua
Oleum essential oils. Local books and
cds. Candles, incense. MC, Visa.

The Health Food Shop
Health food shop

20 Baron Taylor Street, Inverness IV1 1QG
Tel: 01463-233 104
Open: Mon–Sat 9.00–17.30, Sun closed
Website on the way

In the town centre, great for stocking up on wholefoods, they even have spelt bread. Fridge and freezer with vegan cheeses such as Tofutti and Bute Island Sheese, fake bacon, chicken, tofu, vegan Swedish Glace ice-cream. Lots of non-dairy milks such as rice, oat, almond, coconut.
Vegan chocolate by Plamil, Montezuma, Conscious raw, Booja Booja, Organica.
Bodycare by Faith in Nature, Jason, Avalon, Weleda, full Natracare range, some baby stuff.
Supplements by Solgar, Viridian, Vogel, Nature's Aid, Quest, Lifeplan, Lamberts. Weleda and Nelsons homeopathy. Essential oils.
Cleaning by Ecover and six refills, Ecoleaf. Good range of books, some magazines. They can order in anything you need. Also mail order. MC, Visa, Amex.

Holland & Barrett, Inverness
Health food shop

34 Eastgate, Inverness IV2 3NA
Tel: 01463-234 267
Open: Mon–Sat 9.00–17.30,
Sun 10.30–16.30
www.hollandandbarrett.com

Inverness local group
Vegan Inverness
Local social group

www.veganinverness.weebly.com
Facebook: Vegan Inverness

Meet for meals out around Inverness and surrounding towns. They welcome local or visiting vegans or people interested in becoming vegan.

Sky Delights

Vegetarian organic shop & coffee bar

9 Leopold Street, Nairn IV12 4BE
Tel: 01667-452 874
Open: Mon–Sat 9.00–17.00. Sun closed
www.skydelights.co.uk

Officially a vegetarian take-away but they do have four bar stools, and it's a 98% organic wholefood shop too.

The cafe/take-away has homemade soups, filled pitta breads, spelt flour tarts including vegan options. Hot and cold organic sandwiches to order. Homemade vegan cakes, with gluten-free, sugar-free, nut-free and raw options. Organic smoothies, teas, Fairtrade coffees, cold drinks.

The shop has all organic fruit and veg. Findhorn organic breads daily Wed–Sat. Chilled goods with vegan cheeses, meat replacers, their own hummus, vegan yogurts. No freezer. Vegan chocolate by Plamil, Montezuma, Moo Free, Seed & Bean, Booja Booja.

Some bodycare and supplements and they can order in anything you need including Natracare and baby stuff.

Cleaning by Ecover and a couple of small refills. Some Detoxyourworld books.

The owner is a nurse and there is a qualified nutritionist in store a couple of days a week. Cookery and nutrition workshops. Outside catering, bespoke cake orders, specialise in sugar, dairy, wheat and gluten-free. MC, Visa.

Sky Delights tell us places to eat in Nairn include three Indians, Thai, Italian, Chinese, and a new bistro called Thyme which has some vegetarian dishes, lot of gluten-free and dairy-free and can cater for vegans. This seaside town has lots of hotels and B&Bs, and the owners often pop into Sky Delights to get food for their veggie guests.

Wester Hardmuir Fruit Farm

Fruit farm and omnivorous shop

Auldearn, Nairn IV12 5QG
(5 miles east of Nairn on A96)
Tel: 01309-641 259
Open: Jun–Dec every day 9.00–18.00
www.hardmuir.com

Family-run fruit farm near Nairn where you can buy a wide range of fruit and veg picked fresh each morning. In summer you can walk around the farm and pick your own.

In June they have rhubarb and poly-tunnel strawberries, followed by goose-berries (end June); raspberries, black, red and white currant, logan and tayberries, brambles, blueberries; apples and plums (end August). Use their baskets or bring your own. There are some "table-top" strawberries under cover for picking on wet days or by elderly or less abled people.

The farm shop also sells potatoes and, according to season, beans, beetroot, broccoli, cabbage, carrots, cauliflower, leeks, onions, parsnips, peas, sprouts, swedes and turnips. Also oatcakes, home baking, jams, chutneys and more. Picnic and play area.

West Highland Organics

Self-service organic veg stall

25 Argyle Street, Ullapool
Ross-shire IV26 2UB
Tel: 01854 613 265
Open: all year round:
Apr–Oct every day, daylight hours, stall at the house;
Apr–Oct Sat stall at the market in the car park of the Seaforth pub-restaurant;
winter contact the house.
Email: whorganics@gmail.com

Not a shop, it's a house where Simon grows veg, which whilst not officially certified are clearly organic.

In the summer April to end October there's a stall at the house where you help yourself and pay for courgettes, tomatoes, peppers, salad, chard, potatoes etc.

Apr–Oct on Saturdays there is also a market stall 9.00–17.00 in the car park of the Seaforth pub-restaurant. This stall also has home baking and jams.

In the winter the house can still supply salad grown in polytunnels, potatoes, chard, leeks, broccoli.

Since the Troll-Yard wholefood store closed a few years ago, **Costcutter** on West Argyle Street in Ullapool do some wholefoods which they get from Highland Wholefoods. You can also find some in Tesco.

Recommended by local vegetarians for eating out are:
The Ceilidh Place, 12–14 West Argyle St.
The Ferry Boat Inn, Shore St.
The Frigate pizza restaurant, Shore St.
The Argyll pub/hotel at 18 Argyle St, does vegetarian but not vegan food, and won Wester Ross pub of the year 2011. Weekly quiz night, live music in the season, real ales.
And there are a Chinese take-away and "a fantastic though pricey Indian."

Tourist info:
www.ullapool.com

Black Isle Brewery

Vegetarian brewery with tours

Old Allangrange, Munlochy
Ross-shire IV8 8NZ
Tel: 01463-811 871
Open for tours: Mon–Sat 10.00–18.00,
Sun (Apr–Sept only) 11.30–17.00
www.blackislebrewery.com

Organic, vegetarian brewery selling a range of fabulous bottled ales and supplying cask ale to many pubs. The beers are all vegan besides one that contains honey. You can order cases of their bottled ales online, or buy from their shop. Phone to enquire about tours, or just turn up.

Cocoa Mountain, Balnakeil

Vegetarian chocolate cafe and shop

8 Balnakeil Craft Village, **Durness**, Lairg,
Sutherland IV27 4PT (a mile west of Durness)
Tel: 01971-511 233
Open: Easter–Oct Mon–Sun 9.00–18.00,
winter Mon–Sun 11.00–16.00,
closed Dec 25–6, Jan 1–2 and 10–31
www.cocoamountain.co.uk
www.durness.org

Probably the most geographically
remote chocolate producer in Europe, in
the most north-westerly village in
mainland Britain. All the chocolates and
truffles are gluten-free and some are
vegan, including Turkish Delight, and
even a vegan chocolate hamper for £70.
Also vegan hot chocolate, mocha,
organic coffee, cappuccino, latte, teas,
organic cold drinks. Croissants and
biscuits, but not vegan.

Also online store.

Another branch in Auchterarder, Perth.

Islands

The Holy Isle

Vegetarian peace centre with full board and tea room

Lamlash Bay, Holy Isle KA27 8GB
Tel: 01770–601 100
www.holyisland.org
Email: reception@holyisland.org
Tea room open Mar–Oct Mon–Sun 10.00–17.00
Getting there: From the ferry terminal at Ardrossan Harbour take the ferry to Brodick on the Isle of Arran. The journey takes 55 minutes. At Brodick take the number 323 bus to Lamlash Pier (10 minutes) where you board the ferry to Holy Isle. The ferry trip takes about 10 minutes.
Ferries to Arran: www.calmac.co.uk
Holy Isle Ferry:
Tom Sheldon tomin10@btinternet.com or 01770 600 998; or Jim Blakey 01770 700 463 or 07970 771 960

Come here for a course, or just visit the island for a day or two and either stay here or visit their tea room and shop for a drink (but you'll need to bring your own food). The ferry from Arran arrives close to the centre and the tea shop building. In the shop they sell incense, candles, dharma books.

At the north of the island there is the Centre for World Peace and Health, which is linked to the Tibetan Samye Ling Monastery in Dumfriesshire (see that chapter). They offer retreats and courses, and also welcome guests to stay at the Centre for personal retreats or holiday breaks. A closed Buddhist retreat takes place at the south end of the island.

You can also visit Holy Isle for the day. The island is divided into several areas, some of which are reserved for birds and animals, others for a native tree planting programme. Visitors should stay on the paths and not bring animals onto the island.

65 beds in simple yet inviting, fully

furnished rooms with central heating and wash basin. Price per person including three vegetarian meals a day £28 single sex 8-bed dorm, £36 twin, sea view twin and double £42.50, single £47.

Guests are invited – but by no means expected – to join in the daily meditation schedule, and are welcome to enjoy the whole island including the beautiful ornamental Mandala Garden.

No pets or fires on the island. No alcohol, drugs or tobacco. No one under 16 at the centre. MC, Visa.

Allandale House

Omnivorous guest house

Corriegillis Road, Brodick, Isle of Arran KA27 8BJ
Tel: 01770–302 278
Open: Mar–Oct
www.allandalehouse.co.uk

---

10 minutes walk from the ferry to the mainland, and they can give you a ride from here to the ferry for Holy Isle or you can take the bus. 2 doubles ensuite, 2 family ensuite (double and single plus extra bed or cot), 1 triple ensuite, 1 twin with private bathroom opposite and handbasin in room. £40 per person, or £45 single occupancy in double, minimum stay 2 nights, under–13 £18, under–2 free. Cot £10 per stay. Cooked vegetarian breakfast. Some rooms are ground floor.

Lounge with computer, garden,

payphone. Free wifi. High chair. Rooms have tv, tea/coffee making, hairdryer. Private parking. AA 4 stars. The owner can recommend nearby places to eat.

Belvedere Guest House

Omnivorous guest house

Alma Road, Brodick, Isle of Arran KA27 8AZ
Tel: 01770-302 397
Open: all year
www.vision-unlimited.co.uk

2 doubles ensuite, 1 ground floor twin ensuite (disabled access), £30–45 per person; double £25–35; single £25–35. No child discount. Can accommodate babies. Rooms have tea/coffee making, radio, electric blankets, hairdryer. Vegetarian or vegan breakfast. No dogs. Safe deposit, luggage storage, bicycle rental, free wifi. The owners run a nearby seafront restaurant with vegetarian options and there are other nearby restaurants.
In-house aromatherapy, hypnotherapy, reflexology, Reiki, personal development for individuals and corporate groups.

Drimlabarra Herb Farm

Vegan organic herb farm, sanctuary, retreat & herbal medicine centre

Kildonan, Isle of Arran KA27 8SE
Tel: 01770-820 338
www.veganherbal.com

A veganic (stockfree organic) herb farm with fruit orchard and thousands of medicinal trees, established at the south end of Arran by two registered medical herbalists to research health via herbal treatments, diet and hands-on green living. You can come for open days (includes guided herb walk around the farm, vegan food and herb tea tasting), consultations (11.30–15.30, £75

including vegan lunch), residential workshops, apprenticeships and vegan volunteer weeks. Campsite for up to 6 large tents with a caravan. See website for the latest calendar.

Arran tourist info:
www.visitarran.net
www.arran.co.uk
www.scotland-inverness.co.uk/arran

Argyll Hotel

Omnivorous hotel and restaurant

Isle of Iona, Argyll PA76 6SJ
Tel: 01681-700 334
Open: Mar to Oct
Restaurant 08.00–10.00, 12.30–14.00, afternoon tea till 16.00, 19.00–20.30
www.argyllhoteliona.co.uk

16 rooms, price per room with breakfast: 6 double/twin/family ensuite sea view £116-136, 2 double ensuite garden view £78-98, 1 double shared bathroom garden view £60-£75. 6 single ensuite garden view £54-65. 1 apartment ensuite sea view £170-189. Third person in family room £25. Camp beds for under-12 £15, under-4 free. Children in own room 15% reduction. Dogs flat charge £10.
They grow their own organic veg, use Fairtrade, bake bread with nuts, seeds and even berries, and buy from Green City Wholefoods in Glasgow. Rooms have tea making, books and a guide to the island, but not tv or phone. Hairdryer, alarm clock or even spare beach towels available. 4 lounges, tv room with dvd player and computer with broadband. Scottish Tourist Board 3 stars.
Evening restaurant booking essential, always has vegetarian, vegan and gluten-free options. Guests' bar open 11.00–23.00.

Woodwick House

Omnivorous hotel

Small veggie-friendly hotel in the tiny area of Evie. 8 rooms, price per person: one single £45; 2 twins and one double £35 (£45 as single): one twin ensuite and 2 double ensuite £50 (£55 single); one large double ensuite £55 (£65 single).

Breakfast begins with cereal or organic muesli, followed by veggie sausages, tomatoes, mushrooms, baked beans and toast. Soya milk, vegan margarine and vegan muesli are available. They can cater for special diets.

Fri-Sat there is a three-course dinner menu, £28, which is flexible and could start with avocado and rocket gazpacho followed by wild rice pilaf with sauteed spinach and spicy tomato sauce, finishing with plum strudel or pepper poached pears.

Evie is a very special, peaceful place which tends to attract those who care for the environment. Orkney has few trees and has always had a lack of wood, so is full of ancient historical sites which have survived because all the buildings were made from stone. The most impressive ancient monuments are all on Mainland like the Village of Skara Brae, the tomb of Maes Howe and the Ring of Brodgar. The best preserved example of a fortified stone tower in Orkney is only one and a half miles down a track from the area of Evie.

Wildlife is abundant and many people come to birdwatch. There are beautiful walks and sandy beaches nearby.

There are washbasins in the rooms that are not ensuite. Lounge with the only tv in the house, dvd, video, open fire. Function room with baby grand piano (which you can play) for the occasional music and theatre groups, this room is good for writing and drawing. Local artists' work is on display around the house and for sale.

Evie
Mainland
Orkney KW17 2PQ
Scotland

Tel: 01856-751 330
Fax:01856-751 383

www.woodwickhouse.co.uk
mail@woodwickhouse.co.uk

Open: all year

Children welcome and they have cots and high chairs

Dogs are welcome for a fee of £10 for the duration of the stay if they come into the house

Directions: Evie is on the east coast of the largest island, Mainland. Fly to Kirkwall Airport or catch the ferry from Scrabster to Stromness.

Drying room. Storage for outdoor sports equipment.

Wide range of Orkney books, maps and local info

Packed lunches available

Wifi

Parking: available

Two rooms on ground floor

Licensed for civil ceremonies

Scottish Tourist Board 2 stars

Visa, MC +3%

Da Böd Cafe

Vegetarian and vegan cafe by day and restaurant in the evening, the only veggie place in Shetland. Open every summer to raise funds for the adjacent wildlife sanctuary in a stunning location. Down on the seafront at Hillswick. The name means the trading post in Norse.

Food is by donation – pay what you can, and all the proceeds go to help upkeep of the sanctuary.

Wholefood and organic as much as possible, they have snacks and light eats during the day such as soup, filled pitta breads, broccoli and cauliflower bake and pizzas (with vegan option).

Evening meals include summer vegetable and cashew nut loaf, mushroom stroganoff and provencal vegetable plait.

For dessert there is a vegan chocolate cake with hot chocolate sauce and apple and strawberry crumble.

The menu changes as they like to experiment. They can always cater for special diets.

They run various children's projects, raising awareness and educating children on animal and environmental issues and hold story-telling and musical evenings.

Bring your own bottle of wine.

Also an internet cafe by donation.

Shetland

Vegetarian cafe and restaurant (plus B&B)

Hillswick Wildlife Sanctuary
Hillswick
Shetland ZE2 9RW

Tel: 01806–503 348

www.
shetlandwildlifesanctuary
.com

hillswick.wildlife@virgin.net

Sanctuary open most afternoons Jun–Sep but ring first before visiting. Tea, coffee, biscuits available, no charge but donations gratefully accepted.

Cafe open: Jun–Sep
Sat–Sun 11.00.00–17.00

BYO

Children welcome and they have a playroom for them while you're eating, painted out like an underwater cave.

Directions:
Drive from Lerwick on A971 North as far as you can go until you get to Hillswick then turn left down onto seafront.

No credit cards

Foxwood

Foxwood is a new house designed by the owner, standing in 4 acres of land surrounded by magnificent countryside, a blend of mountains and moorland, sea and islands, green fields with sheep and cattle. The house has a magnificent view of the Cuillin mountain range to the south, and of Loch Bracadale and MacLeod's Tables to the north-west. Come for the peace, beauty and quiet or just relax in the big sitting room, which can also be used for dancing, music, story-telling, yoga and workshops.

3 separate areas: large twin ensuite with own lobby; double with large bathroom with sauna, jacuzzi bath and shower; large family ensuite with double and single bed, with lobby and space to prepare snacks. £35 per person, children £20 in family room, no charge for baby.

Breakfast includes fresh seasonal fruit, fruit salad, yogurt, cereals, fruit juices, jams (most sugar-free), brown rolls, Scotch pancakes, oatcakes, vegan hot cross buns and scones, toast, vegan waffles, mushrooms, tomatoes, sausages, beans.

Maps and guidebooks available. The ground is bright with bluebells and primroses in spring, followed by a host of other wild flowers including orchids. Eagles, larks and herons fly overhead. Seals, whales, dolphins and octopus are found in the surrounding waters, and otters on land or water.

Treatments available in the house or nearby include acupressure, aromatherapy, craniosacral therapy, Feldenkrais, holographic repatterning, Human Givens therapy, hypnotherapy, massage, psychotherapy, qi gong, raw food living, reflexology.

The Old School at Dunvegan can do vegetarian food, 15 minutes away by car. The owners of Foxwood are a mine of information on Skye and places to eat vegetarian or vegan.

Vegetarian bed and breakfast

11A Ullinish
by Struan
Isle of Skye IV56 8FD
Scotland

Tel: 01470–572 331

www.scotland-info.co.uk
/foxwood

e-mail: treefox@hotmail.com

Directions: In north-west Skye, 1 hour's drive from the bridge. Follow A850 north towards Portree. At Sligachan turn left onto A863 to Dunvegan. After 15 miles you pass through Struan. Take next turning left which is a single track road signposted for Ullinish. This is a loop road which makes a right angled turn around the Ullinish Lodge Hotel. Continue until you pass a red telephone box on left. A further 50 metres brings you to a track on the right which goes over a cattle grid and on to Foxwood, a quarter of a mile from the sea.

Children welcome, big lounge, games

Pets only if sleeping in car

Internet access available and wifi

Cash, cheque or Paypal

The business is up for sale as a going concern along with a brand new house next door.

The Old Croft House

Come and pamper yourself in a luxury vegetarian bed and breakfast on the dramatic Isle of Skye in the Highlands of Scotland. This 19th century former croft-house is beautifully located next to the River Snizort, with views over the hills and plenty of walks from the door. They are perfectly positioned central to Skye and only 4 miles from Portree, the island's capital, with its range of shops and places to eat.

One double ensuite room from £26 per person, with private patio. You can bring a baby or child at no charge except £2 if they want breakfast. Cot or sleeping bag available.

Breakfast is served in your room so there is no need to rush in the morning. There is an amazing range on the menu, such as home-made American style pancakes with warm syrup, soya vanilla yogurt and mixed berries; homemade granola with soya vanilla yogurt and fruit; traditional fry-up including sautéed potatoes, veggie sausages, roasted tomatoes, field mushrooms and homemade baked beans; or a big bowl of traditional Scottish porridge topped with raisins or served with fruit. All can be made vegan. Vegetarian Guides doesn't normally list non-vegan options, but here the eggs are from a local vegetarian who keeps the chickens as pets after laying. And just to ensure you can never manage lunch there is even toast from their homemade bread, served with homemade preserves. All drinks are Fairtrade.

The Old Croft House is within easy reach of the Cuillin Mountain range, the Quiraing and Old Man of Storr, Skye's most famous walks. They offer help to walkers of all abilities and use of maps.

In Portree are Jacksons Wholefoods store and Arriba, a vegetarian and vegan-friendly bistro.

Isle of Skye

Vegetarian bed & breakfast

6 Carbost
Skeabost, by Portree
Isle of Skye IV51 9PD

Tel: 01470-532 375

www.vegetarianskye.co.uk
Facebook: The Old Croft House Vegetarian B&B on Isle of Skye
skyecrowes@gmail.com

Train station:
Kyle of Lochalsh 39 miles. Good bus service to Portree (4 miles), local buses and taxis from there.

Open: all year

Directions: Take the A87 north leaving Portree signed for Uig for approximately 3 miles. At the first main junction take a left turn onto the A850 signed to Dunvegan and follow this road for 0.5 miles. Take the first turning left onto a minor single track road, go over the cattle grid and it is the next house on the right. See website for map.

Although space is limited, children welcome, facilities for babies include travel cot.

Dogs welcome

No smoking throughout

Parking available

Room has hairdryer, folding table, small fridge, tea/coffee making with snacks, satellite tv, magazines.

Isle of Skye accommodation

Six Willows

Vegetarian bed & breakfast

6/7 Feriniquarrie, **Glendale**, Isle of Skye IV55 8WN
Tel: 01470–511 351
Open: all year
www.sixwillows–skye.co.uk

Double/twin and family room for 3, £25–28 per person. Single use £35–39. Discounts Easter–June, Sep–Dec. Children welcome, cot, high chair.
Huge cooked vegetarian breakfast, vegan no problem. Pets welcome. Rooms have dvd tv (dvds only). Facilities: iron, laundry, hairdryer, wifi.
Extras you can book: back massage, acupressure, meditation, holographic repatterning, evening tray of snacks and dips, deluxe hot chocolate, Fairtrade coffee.
The nearby **Three Chimneys** restaurant does a 7 course vegetarian meal.

A lot of other B&Bs in Skye will do a vegetarian breakfast.
Almost every restaurant on Skye, except some of the seafood places, will provide vegetarian food and can do something vegan.

Isle of Skye – Broadford

The Harbour Restaurant

Omnivorous bistro & coffee shop

Main Street, Broadford, Isle of Skye IV49 9AE
Tel: 01471–822 687
Restaurant open: Thu–Sun 18.30–21.30
www.harbourbroadford.co.uk

Enjoy the view of the bay, watch the birds or the sunset. The owners have both vegetarian and vegan family members and dishes are marked on the menu V or VG, brilliant! Also they use lots of Fairtrade. Only 24 seats so phone ahead to avoid disappointment as they are full every evening in summer.
Here are some vegan dishes: soup with crusty bread £4; spicy chickpea hummus with garlic and ginger £4.50; roast squash with garlic mushrooms, or stuffed with vegetarian haggis £11, served with veg and sautéed potatoes or brown rice; cinnamon oaty crumble with fresh apples or other seasonal fruit £4.50, served with vegan yogurt. Special offer 3 courses £18.
Families welcome. Licensed.

The Old School Restaurant

Omnivorous restaurant

Dunvegan, Isle Of Skye IV55 8GU
Tel: 01470–521 421
Open: Easter–Nov Mon–Sun 18.00–22.00,
school holidays also Wed–Sun 12.00–14.30
(best to check first if open);
winter Fri–Sat only 18.00–21.00;
26 Dec–Mar closed
www.oldschoolrestaurant.co.uk
For more info and bookings phone or email
oldschoolrestaurant@hotmail.com

Just down the road from Dunvegan Castle and housed in the old village school. 2 or 3 starters and mains are vegetarian, more if you tell them you're coming, and can be adapted for vegans, get in touch before booking.

Lunch 2 courses £12.50, 3 £15.95. Evening starters £3.80–4.80 such as soup of the day, green salad, mains £14.50 such as dal stuffed peppers with sweet potato chips; filo pastry parcel stuffed with root veg, caramelised onion and pine nuts, with red wine and redcurrant sauce.

Desserts include for vegans sorbet and fruit salad.

Disabled facilities. Baby–changing. Booking essential especially in summer, it gets busy! MC, Visa.

Also in Dunvegan, Fasgadh Stores community shop and the Fruit and Nut Place have fruit, local veg, wholefoods and flowers.

Tourist info:
www.dunvegancastle.com

Glendale Shop and Post Office

Grocer and post office

2 Lephin, Glendale, Isle of Skye IV55 8WJ
Tel: 01470–511 266
Open: Mon–Sat, Oct–end of May: 11–18.00,
June–Sept: 10–19.00. Closed Sun.
www.glendaleskye.com
p6resthome@btinternet.com

A well-stocked shop that's a hub of the community. Fresh fruit and veg. Wholefoods including tinned and dried pulses. Organic items like tamari, molasses and maple syrup. Silken tofu, soya milk, soya cream. Large range of bread. Linda McCartney frozen sausages and some frozen Indian foods. Vegan cakes.

Some bodycare such as shower gels, Kingfisher toothpaste, Ecover cleaning.

SCOTLAND Islands – Skye

151

Cafe Arriba

Omnivorous bistro/cafe

Gladstone Buildings, Quay Brae, **Portree**
Isle of Skye IV51 9DB
Tel: 01478–611 830
Open:
Easter–autumn Mon–Sun 08.00–22.00;
winter Thu–Sat 08.00–17.00, Sun 10.00–
16.00, Mon–Wed closed;
closed 25–6 Dec, 1–2 Jan
www.cafearriba.co.uk
Facebook: Cafe Arriba

Cafe specialising in breakfast by day
and bistro by night. They are keen on
local and Fairtrade. The blackboard
menus change daily according to who's
cooking and always have vegetarian
dishes and vegan on request.
All day big veggie cooked breakfast
until 16.30. Soups such as hot peppery
broccoli, or sweet potato and cinnamon.
Daily specials £4.25–7.50 such as rich
vegetable goulash with warm flatbread;
or 3 types of hummus (with sun-
blushed tomato hummus, chilli and
garlic, plain) with salad and homemade
bread.

Prince of India

Omnivorous Bangladeshi restaurant

Bayfield Road, Portree, Ise of Skye IV51 9EL
Tel: 01478–612 681
Open: Jul–Sep Mon–Sun 12.00–24.00;
Oct–Jun Mon–Sun 16.30–23.30
www.princeofindia.me.uk

Three course business lunch Mon–Fri
£8.95. Starters and side dishes £3.55.
Veg or mushroom jalfrezi, chilli, balti etc
£5.95–6.95. Rice around £2–3. Take-
aways cheaper.
House wine £2.95 glass, £14.95 bottle.
Children welcome, no high chairs. MC,
Visa.

Ferry Inn Hotel

Omnivorous restaurant & hotel

Uig, Skye IV51 9XP
Tel: 01478-611 216
Open: Mon–Sun 18.00–22.30,
summer also 12.00–14.00;
closed 24-5, 31 Dec, 1 Jan
www.ferryinn.co.uk

Very handy for the ferry to Tarbert (islands of Harris and Lewis) as the terminal is 5 minutes away. One reader found several menu items (£5–9) are vegan such as samosas, spring rolls, 3–bean veggie chilli as well the as ubiquitous jacket spud & beans. Soup £4.15. Specials £6–6.50. Mains lunch £7–11, evening £9–13. The evening menu includes homemade veg curry, penne pasta arrabiata, vegetarian quarter-pounder with side salad and fries; or parsnip, sweet potato and chestnut bake with salad.
Wine £4.50 glass, £14.20 bottle. Children welcome, high chair. Outside seating, dogs welcome there. MC, Visa. **Hotel** has 6 ensuite rooms: 1 single, £46–49; 2 twin, 3 double £40–44 per person, single occupancy £80–88. Children welcome. No dogs. Note that the "leather" lounge seating is actually fake. Two bars.

Getting to Skye:
Train or fly to Inverness and bus to Portree.
Other bus services from London, Glasgow, Edinburgh to Portree.
Bus or train from Fort William to Mallaig, then ferry to Armadale on Skye.
Train to Kyle of Lochalsh via Inverness.
Drive to Kyle of Lochalsh and over the Skye Bridge. Or drive to Mallaig for the ferry to Armadale.
Car rental and cycle hire are available on the island, as well as guided walks and tours.

The Internet Guide to Scotland and the Isle of Skye:
www.scotland–info.co.uk/skye.htm

Information supplied by Foxwood vegetarian B&B.

Uist Wholefoods Cooperative

Wholefood online ordering service

www.uistwholefoods.com

This is not a shop, but a means by which locals and visitors can place monthly wholefood orders from the Highland Wholefoods Cooperative catalogue, with no minimum spend. See website for more details. Covers the Uists from Berneray to Eriskay.

INDEX

Indexes

A–F INDEX

F–I INDEX

INDEX

F–I

J–R INDEX

R–Z INDEX

INDEX R-Z

LOCATIONS INDEX

LOCATIONS INDEX

HELP MAKE THE NEXT EDITION
EVEN BETTER

Please send corrections and new entries to
updates@vegetarianguides.co.uk

and we will post them up at
www.vegetarianguides.co.uk/updates

Buy all Ronny's Scoffer vegan cookbooks at
www.vegetarianguides.co.uk

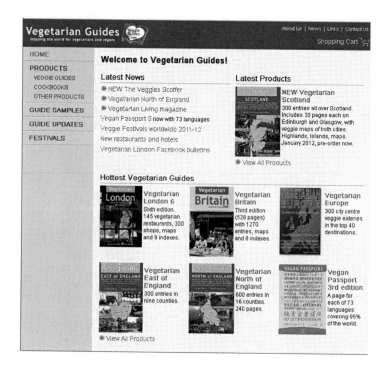

In the same series

600 entries! 240 pages!

Vegetarian North of England covers:
Cheshire
Cumbria
Derbyshire
County Durham
Lancashire
Lincolnshire
Manchester
Merseyside
Northumberland
Nottinghamshire
Tyne & Wear
Yorkshire
Isle of Man

40 pages on the Lake District.
65 pages on Yorkshire.
99 veggie restaurants, cafes and take-aways.
40 city & country pubs, seven 100% vegetarian.
23 vegetarian B&Bs, 40 veg-friendly ones
150 ethnic restaurants with big veggie menus.
Detailed reviews with prices, hours, sample
dishes, plus what's on the menu for vegans.
280 health food and wholefood stores.
Four Indexes for quick reference.
Beer section.
Top 10 places to get you started.
The perfect present for veggies and vegans,
a lifesaver if you travel with one.

£9.95

Vegetarian North of England by Alex Bourke & Ronny Worsey, £9.95
ISBN 978-1-902259-11-6, 240 pp, 8"x5", published by Vegetarian Guides

Available now mail order from Vegetarian Guides, or order through bookshops

www.vegetarianguides.co.uk
Telephone orders 020-3239 8433
(24 hours, we'll call back)

All you need on the road